# THE ENCYCLOPEDIA OF

# NATIVE AMERICA

 >>>>>> TRUDY
GRIFFIN-PIERCE

VIKING

VIKING
Published by the Penguin Group
Penguin Books USA Inc., 375 Hudson Street, New York, New York 10014, U.S.A.
Penguin Books Ltd, 27 Wrights Lane, London W8 5TZ, England
Penguin Books Australia Ltd, Ringwood, Victoria, Australia
Penguin Books Canada Ltd, 10 Alcorn Avenue, Toronto, Ontario, Canada M4V 3B2
Penguin Books (N.Z.) Ltd, 182-190 Wairao Road, Auckland 10, New Zealand

Penguin Books Ltd, Registered Offices: Harmondsworth, Middlesex, England

**3   5   7   9   10   8   6   4**

Library of Congress Catalog Card Number: 94-61491

ISBN 0-670-85104-3

Color separations by Ocean Graphic International Company Ltd.
Printed in China by Leefung-Asco Printers Ltd.

Copyright © Michael Friedman Publishing Group, Inc., New York, 1995
All rights reserved.

Editor: Sharyn Rosart
Art Director: Jeff Batzli
Designer: Lori Thorn
Photography Editor: C. A. Branigan

# ≫ TABLE OF ≪
# CONTENTS

# ≫THE≪
# FIRST AMERICANS

When most non-Indians think of Native Americans, they picture an Indian wearing a feathered headdress, charging across the Plains on horseback to swoop down on innocent settlers or clash with the cavalry. This is how Indians have been portrayed in countless movies, television shows, and books. But this image of the first Americans represents only one type of Indian culture in a very brief period of time from the viewpoint of white America.

The purpose of this book is to show Indians not through the eyes of whites, but through the eyes of Native Americans themselves. History is always written by the victors. North American history has stereotyped the Indians as "savages" whose culture deserved to be destroyed, as "primitives" who needed to be "civilized," and more recently as alcoholics who were not capable of caring for themselves or their people. But Native Americans are much more than a collection of stereotypes. They are people who feel the same range of emotions as other people and who have developed a complex and sophisticated cultural life.

Even the term "Indians" is a misnomer. In 1492, Christopher Columbus, thinking he had landed in the East Indies, called the people he found here "Los Indios," which later became "Indians." No one knows precisely how long these people had been in North America before the arrival of Columbus, but anthropologists and archaeologists estimate that it was at least 30,000 years.

*Opposite: Christina, a young Kickapoo girl, helps her grandmother, Marguerita Salazar, gather firewood near their village at Eagle Pass, Texas. In 1852, a large group of Kickapoo moved to Texas, where some remain today. Above: These Seminole women and children wear European dress instead of traditional patchwork skirts.*

# ⟫ IN THE BEGINNING ⟪

The first people to come to North America may have begun their journey more than 50,000 years ago. The first migrants to America were *Homo sapiens*—humans like ourselves. They traveled from Asia on a land bridge, a broad, flat plain that once linked the two continents across the Bering Sea. Unaware that they were entering a new land, they traveled back and forth across the plain in search of food. Slowly, over the course of many generations and many migrations, they moved across the 1,000-mile (1,600km) -wide bridge, hunting fish and caribou and harvesting what vegetables they could find on the tundra. Always searching for new sources of food, and encountering no competition for either food or shelter, they easily moved across North America.

Eventually the continents shifted and the land bridge was submerged under the ocean. The newcomers continued to spread throughout North and

*Petroglyphs, such as this pictograph of a spirit figure, are evidence of early Americans.*

South America. As they traveled across the vast and varied landscapes of the Americas, families learned to adapt to their new environments. Whether living in the freezing tundra or on the blistering desert, each group learned how to best use the resources at hand to make their clothing, shelter, and hunting and gathering tools.

It was from this period, called the Paleo-Indian period, that we have the first artifacts made by the ancestors of modern Native Americans. Archaeologists first uncovered the primitive tools and weapons in Clovis, New Mexico, and dated the tools back to around 9000 B.C. The weapon points,

named Clovis Fluted points, were also found in the East and Midwest, showing that these toolmakers lived across a wide range of North America.

The points could have been used to hunt animals that are now extinct, such as the woolly mammoth and long-horned bison. Hunting animals this large would have taken the cooperation of a whole family. Later, these family groups began to unite into larger groups of hunters that could kill a herd of animals by stampeding it over a cliff. Such a hunting technique would have required a group of about forty people.

When the last glacial ice covering began to retreat around 8000 B.C., the earth's climate changed drastically. Meadows became deserts and lakes dried up, and the great beasts of the Pleistocene era began to disappear, probably because of their inability to adapt to the changed climate.

This was the beginning of the second era of prehistory, the Archaic period, which lasted until about 1500 B.C. Despite the disappearance of the large mammals, there was still enough game and plant life to support a variety of human societies.

In the western deserts, family bands lived much as their descendants, the Indians of the Great Basin, would: foraging for seeds, bulbs, roots, nuts, and fruit, and hunting waterfowl and rabbits. Catching an antelope would provide a rare but welcome supplement to their diet.

In the East, there was abundant plant life and game, as the woodlands teemed with deer, beavers, rabbits, opossums, squirrels, and turkeys, while the rivers provided plentiful fish, turtles, and shellfish.

In the Mexican Highlands, the first fields were being cultivated. By at least 3000 B.C., the Archaic people planted maize; they also grew pumpkin squash, beans, and amaranth. The practice of cultivating crops spread slowly north from Mexico, until it was common throughout North America.

Corn, beans, and squash became the agricultural mainstays of the tribes in the East, Southeast, Midwest, Plains, and Southwest. Farming made it possible for large numbers of people to live together in towns. No longer entirely dependent on family foraging, a year-round process that had required small groups to travel across large areas searching for food, they could work together on communal fields, growing enough to set aside a surplus for winter. As these farming communities developed into permanent villages, the stage was set for the people to create the complex social systems, cultures, and craft work that distinguished Native American culture.

The Archaic period ended around 1500 B.C. and gave way to the Woodland period, during which the tribes developed pottery and began the custom of building large earthen burial or ceremonial mounds. The best examples of Woodland culture are the Adena-Hopewell peoples, who lived in the Ohio-Kentucky area between 800 B.C. and A.D. 600. The Adena-Hopewell developed large and complex societies with sophisticated ceremonial systems. The Adena-Hopewell built the world's largest serpent effigy: an earthen, coiled snake a quarter-mile (0.4km) long. They also constructed grave mounds that contained well-crafted pottery and jewelry, elaborate carvings, and smoking pipes, which were placed in the mounds as burial offerings to the dead. These mounds were massive, and building them required an enormous amount of work over several generations. Many historians believe that to build such monumental constructions, the

*Anasazi petroglyphs from Cibola National Historic Park at Zuni depict Kokopeli, the humpbacked flute player. In some legends, Kokopeli's hump comes from the seed-filled pack (embodying fertility) he carried on his back.*

Adena-Hopewell must have divided their society into classes: an underclass to build the structures and a nobility to oversee the construction.

The Adena-Hopewell also had a large trading network by which they could acquire raw materials to make crafts. They used obsidian from the Rocky Mountains to shape ceremonial blades. Conch shells, barracuda jaws, and shark and alligator teeth from Florida became beads and necklaces. Carvers shaped mica from North Carolina and Alabama into delicate, shimmering silhouettes of birds and animals. And from the Great Lakes came copper nuggets, which crafters hammered over a hot fire into sheets, then cut into ornaments, rings, knives, and axes.

The Adena-Hopewell culture began to decline in the Midwest and North between A.D. 300 and

*Pueblo Bonito, in Chaco Canyon, New Mexico, was a thriving Anasazi community for nearly four hundred years. The round rooms are remains of ceremonial chambers called kivas.*

900. Some archaeologists believe that the Adena-Hopewell's move to hilltop locations around A.D. 750 was part of a retreat from hostile tribes. The move could also have been due to a change in climate. Wetter weather at this time may have shortened the growing season for maize and made the Adena-Hopewell's old valley sites unlivable.

The last great culture of eastern North America, the Mississippian culture, was probably influenced by the Adena-Hopewell. Like their precursors, the Mississippians were bottomland farmers, cultivating maize, among other crops, and living in compact, well-fortified towns. Originating in the fertile lands of the southeastern river valleys around A.D. 700, this powerful culture spread to Wisconsin, the upper Ohio River, the Georgia coast, Florida, and the lower Mississippi Valley.

The Mississippians were also mound builders. Their towns featured a plaza fronted on one or more sides by flat-topped mounds with a temple or a chief's house on top. The largest temple mound found by archaeologists is in Cahokia in western Illinois. At its height around A.D. 1200, the town housed around 30,000 people within its 15-foot (4.5m) stockade, living in homes made of earth and wood. The temple mound in the town's center stood 100 feet (30.4m) high, on a base that covered 16 acres (6.5ha), an area greater than that covered by Egypt's Great Pyramid. It took thousands of laborers—working without wheels or draft animals —two hundred years to build this massive structure. Built in fourteen stages, the mound contains the tombs of Mississippian nobles. As in Egypt, this society must have relied on a class of slaves to build this structure for the glory of its gods.

The last traces of the Mississippian culture disappeared around 1750, although their society continued to influence many peoples. At about this time, a new influence was also reaching North America: Europeans. This is when our story begins. But to understand the history and culture of the Native Americans, it is important to first understand some things about who they were and are.

# PLACE

"We say 'Nahasdzáán Shimà, Earth, My Mother.' We are made from her," says George Blueeyes, a Navajo elder. You cannot "own" your mother; you cannot divide a member of your family.

Native Americans do not worship the land; they see the land as an expression of the Creator. Treating the earth with the same respect and love that a person shows his or her mother is a way of giving thanks to the Creator for the gift of being alive.

To Native Americans, the earth is sacred, a living entity that exists for the benefit of all forms of life. Indeed, the earth plays a central role in the lives of Indians: "The land is always stalking people. The land makes people live right. The land looks after us," Mrs. Annie Peaches, an Apache elder, told anthropologist Keith Basso.

The idea of dividing the landscape into plots of individually owned land is a concept alien to Native Americans. That is why the Indians could not understand when the Pilgrims built fences to define their property lines. How could anyone own the earth?

Non-Indians tend to think of themselves as separate from the earth; it is something to be mastered. They think in terms of owning land, of land as a commodity. Even the word "frontier" is based on the notion that a certain area lies undeveloped, awaiting settlement and civilization. This implies that land is not good until it is used for some purpose, a belief that is incomprehensible to Native Americans.

*Top: Portrait of a young Lakota man. Above: A Northeastern Indian looks with despair at an industrialized landscape that he no longer recognizes. For Native Americans, such disregard for the earth was incomprehensible.*

For many Indians, certain areas of land hold special significance. For example, the Lakota Sioux call the Black Hills "The Heart of Everything That Is. We say it is the Heart of our home and the home of our Heart," Charlotte Black Elk, a Lakota elder, explained to teacher Ronald Goodman. The Black Hills are sacred to the Lakota and to several other Indian nations, who travel to specific places in these hills for the spiritual regeneration of their people. In the nineteenth century, after the Lakota lost most of their territory to white settlers, the United States government promised that the Indians could keep the Black Hills. But when gold was reportedly found there in 1874, prospectors rushed into the area, completely disregarding Indian treaty rights. Today, whites and Indians are still struggling over ownership of the Black Hills.

*A Navajo woman and her daughter watch their sheep in Monument Valley, Arizona. The Navajo call the land "Nahasdzáán Shimà"— "Earth, My Mother"— and believe it is their sacred responsibility to treat the land with the respect they would accord their mothers, and she in turn will provide for them.*

*Native Americans organized their lives around the cycles of nature: there were times to plant, to hunt, and to gather food. There was also a time to be still and stay inside the lodges, playing games and telling sacred stories.*

# TIME

"Peace...comes within the souls of men when they realize their relationship, their oneness, with the universe and all its powers, and when they realize that at the center of the universe dwells Wakan Tanka, and that this center is really everywhere, within each of us," explains Black Elk, a Lakota medicine man and spiritual leader.

Indians believe that the earth does not need to improve over time; it is beautiful and sacred as it exists at this very moment. Since they view themselves as elements of nature, they organize their lives around the cycle of the seasons. Native Americans recognize the Creator as the power behind these annual cycles as well as the source of all life. All forms of nature are considered sacred and are treated with respect, as one would treat one's relatives. Humans also belong to nature rather than being separate from it.

Traditionally, Native American societies had a time of year to plant; a time to harvest and to give thanks through special rites and celebrations; a time to gather and store food for winter; and, when winter came, a time to stay inside and tell sacred myths and stories. Natural events marked these

times; for example, the reappearance in the night sky in October of the group of stars we call the Pleiades marked the beginning of the Nightway ceremonial season for the Navajo.

With their lives organized around the cycles of nature, Indians have traditionally emphasized living in the present moment, which to them contains both past and future as well. Just as Native Americans live as part of nature, so do they exist in time. For example, instead of thinking about how much timber a forest will yield in the future, they appreciate the trees for their beauty and their contribution to the here and now. They consider the trees separately from the surrounding landscape, but they see all the elements of the landscape as a community living together in the present moment.

In contrast, whites tend to think of time in terms of "progress." They think of themselves as standing on a straight ribbon of time; they can look behind them and see their past, or look ahead and imagine their future. Many non-Indians spend a lot of time worrying about the future, striving for a "better" life.

By focusing on progress, these people think of the natural world in terms of what it will produce for them. They tend to value the world for what they can obtain from it instead of considering that it has a right to remain as it is. By equating progress with goodness, this view separates people from nature, and they eventually forget that they are a part of nature.

This emphasis on progress historically led many whites to see the Native American way of life as inferior. Because our European ancestors believed they were superior to the "primitive" Indians, they felt they had a right—even a duty—to "civilize" the North American continent from coast to coast. In many minds, this belief justified taking Native peoples' lands and destroying their culture. These very different views of time and place held the seeds of all the conflicts to come.

*Opposite: This nineteenth-century lithograph shows two Tohono O'odham women in European dress harvesting cactus fruit. Top:* **Three Deer** *is a painting by Maxine Gachupin of Jemez Pueblo. Left: Mohawk Chief Jake Swamp leads his people in a treeplanting ceremony for the Children's Earth Summit in the spring of 1992. Planting trees is a way of nurturing and honoring the earth, a way of giving thanks for the earth's bounty.*

# ART

*"Spider Woman instructed the Navajo women how to weave on a loom, which Spider Man told them how to make. The crosspoles were made of sky and earth, the warp sticks of sun rays, the heddles [harnesses that guide the threads in the loom] of rock crystal and sheet lightning."*
**—Navajo legend**

The difference between the European and Indian views of the world is also reflected in Indian art. Indians did not create art for art's sake. No traditional Indian would ever paint a picture simply so that it could hang on a wall. In the hundreds of Native American languages, there isn't even a word for "art." As the earth was cherished both for its beauty and for the necessities of life it provided, so the objects the Indians made were both beautiful and useful. If an article was to be used at a feast or celebration, the crafter would lavish special attention on it, decorating it in a fashion appropriate to the spirit of the celebration. Even the objects made for everyday use combined great artistry with utility. Look at the magnificent blankets, pottery, baskets, and clothing pictured in this book, and you will see that in Indian crafts there is no separation between art and life, between beauty and function. The idea of creating art purely for the purpose of viewing and contemplation is alien to Indian thinking. In the Indian worldview, art and life are as one—a unity that pervades Native American culture.

*Native Americans did not create art for art's sake, but combined beauty with utility. Top: A prehistoric Mimbres bowl decorated with a warrior armed for battle. Left: Grace Homer, a Navajo weaver, works a rug on her upright loom.*

## THE ORAL TRADITION

"I think of that mountain called 'white rocks lie above in a compact cluster' as if it were my maternal grandmother," said Benson Lewis, another Apache elder, to anthropologist Keith Basso. "The stories told to me [about that mountain] were like arrows...hearing that mountain's name, I see it....Stories make you live right. Stories make you replace yourself." When he sees the mountain, he remembers the story of the sacred event that happened there. Even when the mountain is not in sight, simply hearing its name brings back the story, which pierces the mind and heart like an arrow, reminding him of the right way to live his life. By living on the right path, people continually restore and regenerate themselves.

When Native Americans first made contact with Europeans, the Indians had a large body of spoken literature. Each tribe had its own collection of folktales, moral fables, and sacred stories that had been passed down verbally from generation to generation. One of the common misconceptions about nonwritten languages is that they are not as highly developed as written languages. Actually, the reverse is often true. Native Americans preserved and retold their stories with great care and precision.

*This 115-year-old Cherokee elder is a keeper of wisdom and history for his people.*

### THE INDIANIZATION OF THE ENGLISH LANGUAGE

Although the English language has changed the lives of Native Americans, they have also changed the English language. When the Europeans arrived, these newcomers saw strange, new things for which they had no names, so they adopted Indian words such as caribou, moose, raccoon, barracuda, manatee, puma, skunk, opossum, chipmunk, mahogany, mangrove, avocado, squash, maize, pemmican, hurricane, chinook, and blizzard. The Europeans also borrowed Native American names for cities such as Chicago, Ottawa, Saskatoon, Seattle, Tallahassee, Tucson, and Winnipeg. Canada's name is derived from an Iroquois word meaning "village." Many states in the United States are named for Indian nations such as the Dakota, the Kansa, the Massachuset, the Illini, and the Utes. Other states' names are translations of Indian descriptions of the land or the water: Iowa means "beautiful land" and Minnesota means "waters that reflect the sky" in Lakota Sioux. Most of the great North American rivers also have Indian names such as Ohio, Mississippi, Missouri, Ottawa, Athabasca, Saskatchewan, Yukon, Suwannee, Mohawk, Catawba, and Potomac.

All Indian cultures greatly valued the ability to speak well before an audience. Leaders were admired as much for their speech making as for their forceful personalities or accomplishments in battle. With no written language, the ability to tell stories well was very important. Folktales and sacred myths showed how the people thought about themselves and their world, what values they held dear. Storytelling was an art, for the stories held the peoples' history, their literature, and their way of life.

The setting for the storytelling was also very important. Indians have always believed in the enormous power of the spoken word; to speak a creature's name is to call it forth. Sacred words must be spoken in a sacred setting and with reverence, to show respect for the creature being summoned.

For many Native American societies, winter was often the time for telling sacred stories. Not only was there more time, because they had finished their harvesting and laid aside winter stores of food, but also—and more important—they could speak of many creatures in nature, holy beings, because those creatures were not present and therefore could not be summoned. This is why the Navajo only tell stories about bears in winter—when the animals are hibernating.

*Above: Acoma potter Ivan Lewis created this storytelling figure. Left: These Sioux Ghost Dance dolls date from the late 1800s.*

*Catholic missionaries had no conception of the complexity of Native American spirituality, but simply saw Indians as heathens to be converted.*

Because their languages were unwritten, the Indians could not understand the whites' reliance on written documents. Such written words were meaningless to them, which is why they did not understand the consequences of signing a treaty. As we have seen, the concept of owning land was alien to the Indians; because writing on paper meant nothing to them either, they signed away their rights to the land without realizing what they were doing. These differences in understanding meant that Indians were easy to cheat. Without a written language, they relied on spoken promises from white leaders; the Indians, masters of verbal skills, had a perfect memory for what the whites had said about a treaty.

Today, many of the remaining Native American languages have been written down. When Christian missionaries went to convert the Indians, one of their frequent first tasks was creating an alphabet and a written form of the native language.

Sometimes Indians who share a language do not share a culture because over the centuries tribes broke up and branches migrated to other parts of the continent, where they developed different habits. Sometimes they adopted aspects of their new neighbors' languages. Today there are about 150 Native American languages still spoken north of Mexico; at the time of European contact there were over 200. Many of the remaining languages have been written down and are still being taught.

Each chapter of this book begins with a quotation from a native leader so that readers can share the power of their expressive words. These passages are meant to be read aloud, as Native Americans would have spoken and heard them.

# NATIVE AMERICAN LANGUAGES

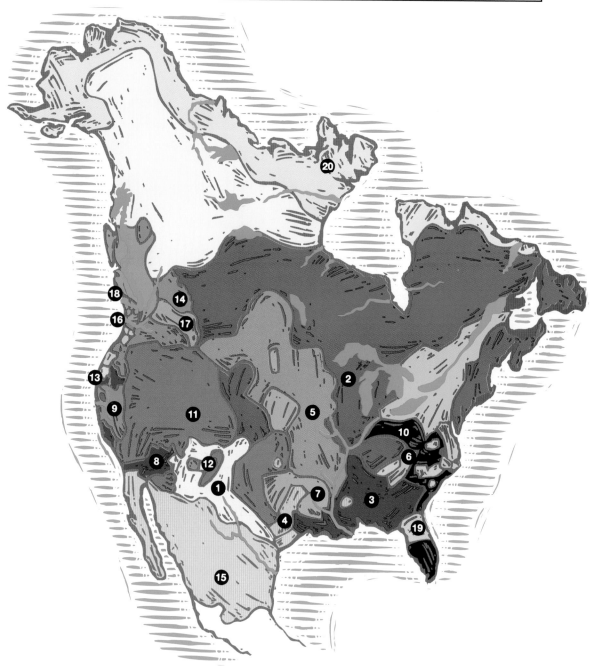

1.  Na-Dene
2.  Algonquian
3.  Gulf
4.  Tonkawa
5.  Siouan-Yuchi

6.  Iroquoian
7.  Caddoan
8.  Hokan-Coahuiltecan
9.  Penutian
10. insufficient data

11. Aztec-Tanoan
12. Keves
13. Yukian
14. Kutenai
15. Karankawa

16. Chimakuan
17. Salish
18. Wakashan
19. Timucua
20. Eskimo-Alea

*Because Native American peoples developed languages before they moved to new locations, the speakers of similar languages live in widely scat-* *tered areas of North America. This map summarizes the major language groupings of North America and where they are spoken.*

# ≫ CULTURE AREAS ≪

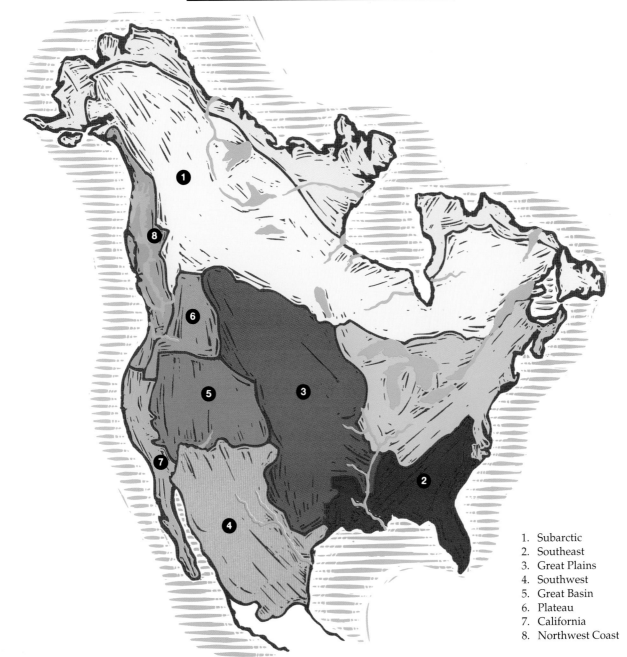

1. Subarctic
2. Southeast
3. Great Plains
4. Southwest
5. Great Basin
6. Plateau
7. California
8. Northwest Coast

*One way to understand the enormous complexity of the American Indian is to use "culture areas." A culture area is a geographical area whose inhabitants share certain traits. The people who live outside this culture area do not share these traits. For example, the various peoples of the Southeast farmed more and had denser populations and a more developed class system than the people of the Northeast. These shared qualities differentiated the Southeastern tribes from their neighbors.*

*The culture areas that are described in **The Encyclopedia of Native America** include the Northeast, the Southeast, the Great Plains, the Great Basin and Plateau, the Northwest Coast, California, and the Southwest. Because it is impossible to portray all the groups in each culture area, a fairly typical group (or groups) is described for each area.*

# CHAPTER ONE

# >THE<
# NORTHEAST

*The Onondaga [Iroquois]...shall open each council....They shall offer thanks to the earth where people dwell—*

*To the streams of water, the pools, the springs, and the lakes; to the maize and the fruits—*

*To the medicinal herbs and trees, to the forest trees for their usefulness, to the animals that serve as food and who offer their pelts as clothing—*

*To the great winds and the lesser winds; to the Thunderers; and the Sun, the mighty warriors; to the moon—*

*To the messengers of the Great Spirit who dwells in the skies above, who gives all things useful to men, who is the source and the ruler of health and life.*

*Then shall the Onondaga...declare the council open.*

*Iroquois Constitution*

# LANGUAGES OF THE TRIBES OF THE NORTHEAST

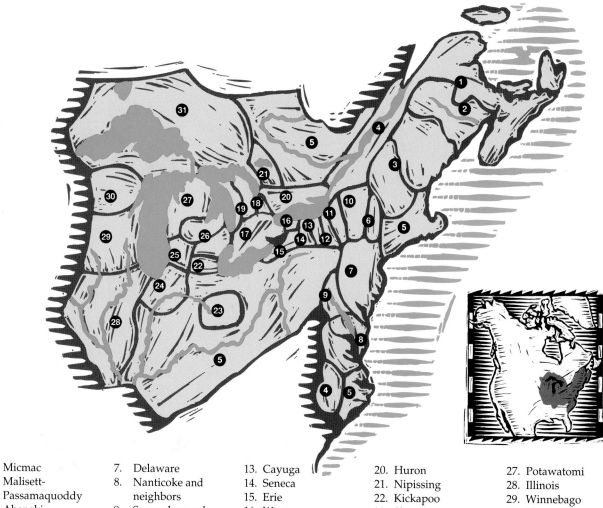

| | | | | |
|---|---|---|---|---|
| 1. Micmac | 7. Delaware | 13. Cayuga | 20. Huron | 27. Potawatomi |
| 2. Malisett-<br>   Passamaquoddy | 8. Nanticoke and<br>   neighbors | 14. Seneca | 21. Nipissing | 28. Illinois |
| | | 15. Erie | 22. Kickapoo | 29. Winnebago |
| 3. Abenaki | 9. Susquehannock | 16. Wenro | 23. Shawnee | 30. Menominee |
| 4. Iroquoian | 10. Mohawk | 17. neutral | 24. Miami | 31. Ojibwa |
| 5. Algonquian | 11. Oneida | 18. Petun | 25. Mascouten | (Chippewa) |
| 6. Mahican | 12. Onondaga | 19. Ottawa | 26. Sauk and Fox | |

The Iroquois-speaking tribes of the Northeast lived around the lower Great Lakes (Lakes Huron, Erie, and Ontario), the St. Lawrence River, and Lakes Champlain and George in what are now parts of Quebec and Ontario in Canada and upstate New York and adjacent Pennsylvania in the United States. Although many tribes spoke Iroquois, those of the Iroquois League—the Mohawk, Oneida, Onondaga, Cayuga, and Seneca—are probably the best known.

The Algonquians lived in two main areas: along the east coast of the Atlantic Ocean and around the western Great Lakes. When the French, English, and Dutch colonists arrived, they met the Algonquian tribes of the east coast: the Abnaki, Wampanoag, Mahican, Narraganset, Penobscot, Powhatan, and Pequot. The Delaware tribes covered a region reaching north and west far beyond the present state's boundaries. Such Algonquian tribes as the Ojibwa (also called Chippewa), Sauk, Fox, Potawatomi, and Menominee also lived in the Great Lakes area. The Winnebago, who lived around Lake Michigan, spoke a Siouan language.

When Indian nations from the East gave up their homelands to the whites in later centuries, they pushed some Algonquians out of Minnesota and onto the northern Plains, where they gave up their town lifestyles to become hunters of buffalo. These nations eventually became the Arapaho, the Cheyenne, and the Blackfeet.

The Indians of the Northeast were among the first Americans to meet the explorers and settlers who crossed the Atlantic from Europe. The native peoples of this region influenced the newcomers in many ways. They showed the settlers how to survive in the new and unfamiliar land, how to hunt, what

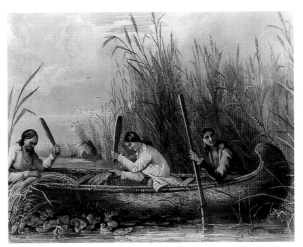

to pick, and what to plant. Nearly half the varieties of vegetables commonly grown in North American gardens today were first planted by these Indians. The Northeastern tribes also left another important legacy. They provided the founding fathers of the United States with some of the guiding prin-

ciples behind American democracy.

When European traders began to arrive on the Atlantic Coast of North America in the first half of the seventeenth century, the Northeast had been home to many Indian nations for thousands of years. Algonquian-speaking tribes extended from the seacoast to the Mississippi River, while Iroquoian-speaking Indians lived in the forests around Lakes Huron, Erie, Ontario, Champlain, and George. The Winnebago, who lived around Lake Michigan, spoke a Siouan language but lived like their Algonquian neighbors.

*Top: Ojibwa girls harvesting wild rice. Above: Governor Durnet meets with the Indian sachems in Albany, New York, during the summer of 1712. The native leaders brought beaver skins for the governor's new bride.*

# THE IROQUOIS

The Iroquois tribes (Onondaga, Cayuga, Oneida, Mohawk, and Seneca) lived in the midst of the largest deciduous forest in North America. This magnificent forest contained elm, hickory, maple, and beech trees, interspersed with stands of hemlock and white pine. The forest gave the Iroquois life: its animals provided food and clothing and its plants and trees furnished food, medicines, and shelter. From logs and bark the Iroquois made canoes, weapons, cooking utensils, and built the homes that gave them their name, *Haudenosaunee,* "The People of the Longhouse."

But the living forests, flowing rivers, and sky-reflecting lakes of the landscape supplied much more than food and shelter to the Iroquois; these natural surroundings provided spiritual sanctuary and replenishment as well. Like all Native Americans, the Iroquois felt a deep spiritual connection to the natural world that surrounded

them. This link was expressed in every aspect of Iroquois life.

For example, when an Iroquois man hunted a deer, he concentrated on becoming one with the spirit of the deer. By identifying with the deer on this deep level, the hunter was able to track it more accurately and, once he had caught it, to treat it with respect. He first knelt beside the animal and thanked it for providing food and clothing for his family. He addressed the deer in a gentle and reverent voice as a beloved friend. Only after praying that the deer's spirit might be reborn and blessed with a long life and a plentiful supply of good leaves and water did he remove his skinning knife from its sheath. After whites arrived, one quality the Iroquois found most appalling about these newcomers was their barbaric behavior after they shot a deer. They rushed out to kick it to see if any life remained, then butchered it immediately, robbing the deer of all its dignity.

*Portraits of Not-to-way (left), an Iroquois chief, and his wife, Chee-a-ka-tchee (above), by American painter George Catlin.*

# THE IROQUOIS YEAR

The Iroquois sense of oneness with the natural world led them to mark the passage of time by the cycles of nature, both on a daily and a seasonal basis. Certain activities occurred at the same time each day or year. For example, every morning, the Iroquois arose at dawn to thank the Creator that they were still alive. Each autumn, Iroquois families left their homes to hunt; then, after the constellation known as the Pleiades reached its zenith, or highest point, at dusk, the hunters packed the meat that had been smoked and dried and returned to their villages. On the fifth night of the next new moon, they held the great Midwinter Rites, a ceremony performed to give thanks, to renew old dreams, to reveal new dreams, and to fulfill the ceremonial obligations envisioned in these dreams.

Winter was a time of bitter cold, during which the Iroquois stayed in the warmth of their longhouses, eating stored maize, vegetables, nuts, fish, and some animals. As spring approached, hunger often plagued them, forcing them to borrow grain from other villages. As winter gave way to spring, two moons from the midwinter moon, the people went out into the maple tree groves to tap the trees and draw out the sap, for which they gave thanks to the forest, especially to the maple trees. They boiled down the sap to make syrup and sugar. Soon flocks of passenger pigeons and other birds returned from their winter migrations to roost in the beech woods. The people netted these pigeons on the hillsides and poked squabs out of their nests, thankful for yet another source of food. As the weather warmed, the men fished with spears and basket traps while women gathered spring greens such as milkweed, poke, leek, and skunk cabbage.

Once the white oak leaves were the size of a red squirrel's foot, it was time to plant seeds of corn, beans, and squash, crops known as the "three sisters" because they were considered siblings of the women who cultivated them. The women soaked

*Contemporary sculpture from the Schoharie Museum of the Iroquois Indian.*

the seeds for several days in an herbal mixture intended to ward off crows, blessed the seeds, and returned them to the earth. The men helped to clear the fields, but it was the women who stirred the corn hills with wooden spades and planted the seeds. In addition to the three sisters, they also planted sunflowers and tobacco.

The month of June saw the appearance of the Berry Moon, named for the ripening of the strawberry. At this time the Iroquois celebrated the first fruit. This was also the time when the bark peeled easily from the trees, enabling men to build homes, repair stockades, and work elm bark into utensils and canoes. The women used this time to tan deerskin to make clothing: first, they prepared each hide by soaking and scraping it; then they tanned the hide by rubbing it with a mixture of animal brains, liver, and fat to smooth and soften the skin. The clothing they made included moccasins, which everyone wore, plus breechcloths for the men and skirts for the women. Men cut their hair in cockscomb scalp-locks by shaving the sides of the head to leave a ridge of hair on top and down the back, while women braided their hair.

In summertime, as their crops grew, the Iroquois held ceremonies to address the most important danger of the growing season. Through

**The Iroquois Snowshoe Dance at First Snowfall** *by George Catlin.*

the prayers of the Thunder rite, they asked the sun, the elder brother and patron of war, not to scorch the earth. "May our grandfathers of the rumbling voices who come from toward the sunset water the three sisters." In honor of the sun, men danced the war dance and played a game known as the hoop and pole game, which symbolized the spearing of the rolling sun. Women and a few old men hoed the corn for the second and third time.

When the three sisters had matured, the women harvested the crops, shelled them, and stored them in barns. At the next moon, everyone gathered together to celebrate the harvest. The Iroquois returned their thanks that the cycle was complete and that they had lived to see it. One Iroquois tribe, the Seneca, prayed: "Great Spirit in heaven, we salute thee with our thanks, that thou hast preserved so many of us another year, to participate in the ceremonies of this occasion." The

people danced and the women sang, "The three sisters are happy because they are home again from their summer in the fields."

Soon the leaves turned red and fell, marking the season when the group of stars known as hunter with his dogs (which we call Ursa Minor) rounded the North Star, Polaris, overtook the bear (Ursa Major), and killed him. As the days grew shorter and colder, the people added warmer clothes: leggings, long-sleeved jackets, and bearskin or rabbit fur robes. It was then that families left their communal longhouses to hunt in the deep woods for venison. The deer, the source of life at this time, was the symbol of men's labor and the emblem of the chiefs. With the coming of deep snow, hunting became more difficult except on snowshoes. Then it was time to return from the winter hunt, ending the yearly cycle with the celebration of the Midwinter Rites to renew the tribe's spiritual ties.

# THE PEOPLE OF THE LONGHOUSE

A typical *Haudenosaunee* longhouse was about 25 feet (7.6m) wide; its length ranged from 80 to 200 feet (24.3 to 60.9m), depending upon the number of families it housed. The Iroquois used logs to build their longhouses in an east-to-west direction and covered the outside with horizontal strips of elm bark. In the longhouse's shadowy interior, the only light came from smoke holes left in the roof or through the doorways situated at either end. When it snowed or rained, the families inside closed sliding panels across the smoke holes, filling the longhouse with eye-stinging smoke and the smells of cooking food, bear's grease, babies, tobacco, soot, and sweat.

The longhouse was home to several families. A typical longhouse held three to five fires, each of which was shared by two families of five or six persons. With every new fire, the Iroquois added two apartments of about 25 feet (7.6m) to the length of the longhouse. Each apartment consisted of a low, wide platform built about a foot (30.4cm) off the ground to avoid the damp and fleas. The people covered the platform with reed mats or thick bearskin rugs for sleeping or sitting. Apartments were open to the central corridor, where each family shared a fire with the family living directly across from them. This central corridor was where the people lived when they were not outside:

## THE FALSE FACE SOCIETY

**D**uring Iroquois ceremonies, special, often secret societies led curing ceremonies to help with particular problems. One such group, the False Face society, wore wooden masks that were carved to represent certain spirits. The False Face members carved these masks into living trees so that the trees' spirits could help in the curing. As they carved, they addressed prayers to the spirit forces. When it was time to cut the mask free, they burned tobacco as an offering. After these activities, the particular kind of spirit being evoked was revealed to the maker, who then painted the mask appropriately and arranged horsehair on it.

women cooked food and pounded their corn in deep wooden containers, people ate and visited, and children played.

Families stored their pots, kettles, weapons, and cradleboards on shelves under the eaves, over their sleeping bunks. They kept corn, tobacco, robes, snowshoes, baskets, and other food and clothing in large bark bins that separated apartments, or in storage areas below the sleeping platforms.

Most Iroquois settlements had from 30 to 150 longhouses, which were built inside a palisade (a fence made of stakes) for protection. The Iroquois generally built their settlements on a rise of land near a stream that they could use for canoe transport, fishing, and drinkable water.

*An Iroquois long-house. Made of seasoned elm bark over a framework of elm-wood poles, the longhouse could house between six and ten families.*

*A group of Seneca Indians pose in front of a longhouse, Cattaraugua Reservation, New York.*

Inheritance in Iroquois society was passed down through the women, who owned, controlled, and continued to live in the longhouse in which they were born. When a man married, he left the longhouse where he had grown up to live in the longhouse of his wife and her family. His only possessions were his weapons, clothing, and the personal objects he brought with him. Iroquois women owned everything else.

The elder women of the longhouse were its leaders, who could appoint and dismiss their longhouse representatives. Such female control was practical because men were gone for such long periods of time. When they were not hunting and trading, men were away for days and months waging war. Women had to run their households and communities as they did the planting and harvesting and raised children. The women of a family group worked together to cultivate crops, sharing gardening tools and plots. Hard work yielded impressive results: it is estimated that each year Seneca women brought in more than a million bushels of corn, along with tons of beans, squash, and sunflower seeds.

## THE LEAGUE OF THE IROQUOIS

During the two centuries from about 1400 to 1600, the Iroquois created a governing body for all their tribes. This was a time when the Indians of the Mohawk Valley were fighting among themselves. Warfare was considered an honorable pursuit for Iroquois men, and warriors enjoyed high status among their people. Although there were many reasons why men went on the warpath, revenge being perhaps the most common, the booty they brought back showed how skillful and brave they had been. The desire for prestige often led to the warpath, for a proven war leader was able to amass a large following that gave him power and status.

Each Iroquois group considered itself to be an independent nation, and bloody feuds between nations were commonplace. According to old Iroquois custom, when a man killed someone, a member of the dead person's family was then entitled to kill the murderer or one of his relatives. A blood feud or "little war" resulted when the murdered person belonged to another Indian nation. As the various Iroquois nations fought among themselves through time, their population declined.

This is why the League of the Iroquois stands out as such a remarkable achievement: after a history of bloodshed, the member nations turned away from war and learned to settle their differences peacefully with fair representation for each group.

According to various Iroquois accounts, the League was founded by Deganawidah, a Huron prophet, philosopher, and mystic, and Hiawatha (not the imaginary Ojibwa hero of Longfellow's poem), an Onondaga orator, worker of magic, and reformer. Deganawidah was inspired to create a unified government but could not communicate his ideas well; Hiawatha's goals were unfocused but he was a powerful and compelling orator. Both had been persecuted and exiled by their people.

One day Deganawidah had a powerful vision of a great spiritual tree of peace, a majestic spruce that touched the sky and had five roots that grew deep into the earth. He saw this spiritual tree of peace as a symbol that represented humanity as it was nourished by the soil of three sets of principles of living: health of body and sanity of mind (represented by peace between individuals and groups); righteousness in thought, speech, and behavior (represented by justice and equity among peoples); and civil authority and physical strength (represented by the power of the sacred force that bound all living things). In his vision, a snow-white carpet covered the base of the spruce and the entire countryside, symbolizing the protection of the lands of the Iroquois people who adopted these guiding principles; all the peoples of the earth could also adopt these principles and thus prosper. A far-seeing eagle perched atop the tree to guard the safety of the peace. Deganawidah saw that the five roots that anchored the tree represented the Five Nations of the Iroquois: the Onondaga, the Cayuga, the Oneida, the Mohawk, and the Seneca.

Hiawatha carried Deganawidah's principles for unified government to the Five Nations. At first the Five Nations met the plan with great resistance because no tribe wanted to give up its independence and freedom. Deganawidah and Hiawatha refused to give up their crusade, however, until they finally convinced each nation to accept the Great Peace. After each tribe accepted the plan, they called a great council of all the chiefs to agree upon the laws of the new Confederacy. They decided that on all issues, the chiefs in the council of the League had to reach unanimous agreement; thus, any chief could veto a proposal. Those who signed the treaty exchanged wampum (shell beads strung or woven into belts that had high symbolic value to the Iroquois) to show that they were sincere about keeping their word.

*Hiawatha, the Onondaga orator who, with the Huron prophet Deganawidah, was instrumental in the founding of the League of the Iroquois.*

# TECUMSEH

*A nineteenth-century etching of Tecumseh.*

Tecumseh (1768–1813) was one of the most visionary Native American leaders. A Shawnee war chief and statesman, he was skilled in diplomacy and dreamed of building an independent Indian nation that would be respected by the whites. Traveling the East from Florida to the Great Lakes, he urged the tribes to unite and work together so that they could keep their land. Tecumseh said, "A man could no more sell land than he could sell the sea or the air that he breathes."

The governor of Indiana, William Harrison, tried to evict all Indians from the Northwest Territory by successfully attacking Tecumseh's headquarters during his absence. Despite this defeat, Tecumseh did not give up but instead joined the British, who were backing Indian alliances against American expansion in the War of 1812. Tecumseh recognized that the price of American freedom was Indian freedom; he hoped to balance American demands for Indian lands with a British presence in America. His hope for a separate Indian nation died with the British defeat.

Tecumseh was respected by both whites and Indians for his character. He spared captives and never slaughtered noncombatants, urging other Indians to win the respect of the whites by following this humane approach.

*A wampum belt was a traditional symbol of diplomatic and ceremonial relationships among peoples of the Northeast. The word is derived from the Algonquian* **wampumpeag**—*cylindrical shell beads.*

The new doctrine of peace promoted the message that blood feuds should stop because all men are brothers. Before the formation of the League, the murder of an individual from another tribe often resulted in war. Deganawidah and Hiawatha proposed that instead of wreaking bloody revenge for killing, men's hearts should be lifted up by a condolence ceremony, in which gifts such as wampum would be paid to the family whose member had been murdered. This arrangement was not intended to devalue human life by setting a price on it; rather, it was a reminder that further killing could not restore the life of the lost loved one, and that peace and the continuation of life were more important.

The Iroquois viewed the lands occupied by their member nations (and sometimes the entire continent) as a symbolic longhouse with each group representing part of the larger family. The villages of the Five Nations were arranged in an east-to-west geographic line just as the families and their fires were arranged in an ordinary longhouse. From east to west were the Mohawks (the Keepers of the Eastern Door of this symbolic longhouse), the Oneida, the Onondaga, the Cayuga, and finally the Seneca (the Keepers of the Western Door). In 1722, the Tuscarora, pushed out of what are now the Carolinas by white settlers, also joined the League, creating the Six Nations. These Six Nations totaled about a dozen villages; each village averaged perhaps 500 persons, and estimates of the total population vary from 1,600 to 6,000.

Fifty representatives called *sachems* from each of the five member nations made up the governing council of the League. Each sachem position had specific duties. Although sachems were always male, they were selected by the clan mothers, and a woman could act in place of a boy who was too young to fulfill his duties. Each member had an opportunity to speak at council meetings and decisions were unanimous.

The League combined a strong confederacy with a skillful use of geography. The Iroquois villages in what is now upstate New York and southern Ontario and Quebec were protected by mountains threaded by rivers that were a major route to the beaver grounds of the south and west. In the late 1500s, the French began to trade with the Huron Indians on the St. Lawrence River and the Algonquian peoples of the Great Lakes. From this trading network the French excluded the Iroquois, who were longtime enemies of both the Algonquians and the Huron. Because the Iroquois controlled Lake Ontario, their competitors were forced to take a longer, more northerly route to reach the French trading posts on the St. Lawrence River.

In years to come, the Iroquois became implacable enemies of the French, as well, and sided with the British throughout the conflicts between the

## THE BOY SCOUTS

*Mr. and Mrs. Ernest Thompson Seton.*

Ernest Thompson Seton (1860–1946) grew up in Canada's eastern woods and western prairie. In 1902, he founded boys' clubs that he called Woodcraft Indian societies. Seton admired Tecumseh, the Shawnee leader, and through the Woodcraft Indian movement tried to teach boys Tecumseh's virtues—honesty, helpfulness, dignity, and kindness. In order to learn self-reliance, the boys organized themselves into self-governing tribes, each with their own animal or plant totem. From the Plains Indians, who awarded "coups" for warriors' courageous deeds, Seton took the idea of counting coup (see Chapter 3, page 81). To minimize competition and encourage individual effort, boys won a feather and a wampum badge for tracking an animal or making a tipi. When Lord Baden-Powell created the Boy Scout organization in England in 1908, he borrowed Seton's basic idea but stripped away the Indian qualities, instead emphasizing more military characteristics. When the Boy Scouts spread to North America, however, Seton added the influence of the Woodcraft Indian movement to give the American Scouts a less military and more Indian orientation.

## ARTS AND CRAFTS OF THE NORTHEAST

*Above: This Wampanoag wooden ladle with bird's head dates from 1681. Below: Onondaga male and female corn husk dolls.*

Traditionally, the peoples of the Great Lakes decorated their clothing with dyed porcupine quills. They made dyes from plants and sewed the brightly colored quills onto leather in the shape of triangles and flowers. In the 1600s the French traders introduced beads and cloth, and groups such as the Ojibwa began using the beads to create intricate floral designs on black velvet. The Iroquois also worked with beads to produce lacy designs in white beads on dark cloth.

The Iroquois are best known today for the wooden masks known as false faces, which are used in curing ceremonies. False faces are still carved from living trees whose spirits are believed to aid in the healing process. The Iroquois continue their tradition of wood carving by making spoons, stirring paddles, bowls, and canes. In some tribes, the women also make splint baskets and corn husk dolls and masks in the old style.

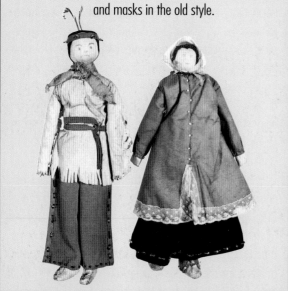

Europeans. As the League developed, the Iroquois practiced warfare against the French in a series of conflicts that actually strengthened the League by drawing the member nations together to fight the outsiders. However, when the American Revolution broke out, the members of the League could not reach a unanimous agreement on whether they should side with the British or the Americans. In a symbolic gesture, they covered the council fire of the League in 1777, which allowed each nation to follow its own path during the war. This division of allegiance effectively ended the League's military power—at a time when settlers had begun to expand westward.

The League of the Iroquois was probably the most successful tribal alliance of any kind, and its principles greatly influenced the founding fathers of the United States. Benjamin Franklin, one of the authors of the American Constitution, drew direct inspiration from the Iroquois League for the Albany Plan of Union for the colonies in 1754. He reminded the colonists, "It would be a strange thing if [the] Six Nations [of the Iroquois] should be capable of forming [and executing] a scheme for such a union...and yet that a like union should be impractical for ten or a dozen English colonies, to whom it is more necessary...."

The Iroquois confederation maintained the power and strength of the Six Nations against all enemies until the American Revolution, when its political institutions were reborn, in part, in the new governments that the whites were establishing for themselves. To European and American philosophers, as well as colonial leaders, the League represented the more just and humane forms of government that they had been seeking. The essence of the League—a humanitarian vision of universal peace and brotherhood—inspired its Iroquois founders long before the arrival of the whites and continues today to guide such organizations as the United Nations. Today the remaining Iroquois people have revived the League of the Iroquois.

*A typical Algonquian village. The men share a pipe while the women go about their daily tasks, skinning a deer, grinding corn, and weaving.*

## THE ALGONQUIANS

Many Algonquians lived north of the Iroquois, in lands where white birch trees were so plentiful that the light of the noonday sun barely reached the forest floor. Coniferous forests covered the slopes of hillsides and mountains, their trees crowded together in dark, spiky cones. Near the rocky, barren tops of mountains, trees bent by the wind clung to life in the thin soil.

But it was the sacred birch trees that took care of the northern Algonquian peoples by providing a building material superior to elm that they used for their homes, canoes, and utensils. The people built conical and dome-shaped wigwams by bending birch saplings and tying their ends together with basswood strips or leather thongs to make a framework. They then covered this framework with mats, skins, or long slabs of birch bark. The canoes that the Algonquians constructed from birch bark were exceptionally light and maneuverable.

## ALGONQUIAN POEM

We are the stars which sing,
We sing with our light;
We are the birds of fire;
Our light is a voice;
We make a road for the spirits,
For the spirits to pass over.
Among us are three hunters
Who chase a bear.
There was never a time
When they were not hunting.
We look down on the mountains
This is the song of the stars.

Algonquians also carved birch bark to record their dreams, memories, and rituals. Women captured haunting designs from their dreams, talking to the images as they created them. They fashioned the birch bark into needle cases, cooking pots, and cutouts shaped in the form of animals and people, each an expression of the living universe. Men inscribed birch-bark memory scrolls with symbols for song sequences and sacred stories. Birch bark thus became a medium for recording knowledge and expressing inner visions.

Like the Iroquois, the Algonquians fit their lives into nature's seasonal cycles, always remembering that the earth was their source of life and that they must nurture both their spiritual and physical selves by giving thanks. When hunters killed, they approached the dead animal with the prayer, "We are sorry to kill you, our brother, that we might live. We do honor to your strength and speed and thank you for the gift of your life."

The Micmac people of southern Nova Scotia and Maine, the northernmost eastern Algonquians, began their annual cycle at the time when the rivers froze. This was a period of cold, snow, and isolation, when families left the village in small groups to hunt. At the time when Bears Retire to Hollow Trees, men wearing snowshoes hunted in pairs to stalk large game with stone-tipped lances or arrows. If the hunters successfully called the spirits of the animals, they might bring back moose or elk and there would be feasting in the lodges of their families. From February, known as the Moon of Snow-blinding, until the middle of March, the men joined together in larger groups for the great hunt for beavers, otters, moose, bears, and caribou.

*An Algonquian wigwam, covered with mats and skins.*

*An Algonquian woman lashes saplings together to make the framework for a wigwam. Behind her, another woman finishes covering a wigwam with skins.*

As the sun began to travel northward, the world renewed itself with fresh signs of life. The rivers flowed with newly melted snow, and by the middle of March the fish began to spawn, often so abundantly that streams swarmed with them, providing yet another source of food. The forests were alive with the cries of birds returning from their winter migrations. The loud honking of hundreds of geese filled the still air, and the people watched with wonder as they flew with orderly precision across the sky, slowly settling gracefully into the lakes. In April, the Moon of Egg-laying, it was time to gather herring, sturgeon, salmon, and Canada goose eggs.

From May, the Moon of Young Seals, until the middle of September, the Moon of Moose Calling, was a time of easy living when the people always had plenty to eat. The sun's return was a gift and everyone enjoyed the longer, warmer days of June, the Moon of Leaf Opening. The people leisurely fished for cod and collected shellfish along the coast. Berries and other summer fruits ripened by August, the Moon when Young Birds Are Full-fledged. With

September came the first frost, heralding the return of winter, and it was once again time to leave their friends and scatter in smaller winter hunting groups.

Farther west in Ontario, Minnesota, Wisconsin, and Michigan, Ojibwa hunters traveled as far away as a hundred miles (160km) from their base camp. The dense canopy of conifers filtered out the sunlight needed for the undergrowth favored by deer, so that the game in these deep woods was a mixture of moose, caribou, and bear. The men had to leave their families in camp to go on long, solitary journeys to hunt in deep snow and heavy storms. Ojibwa religion focused on the larger game animals. The hunter developed a spiritual connection with the woodland caribou, with the moose, and with the bear as he followed their tracks in the bitter cold and ice of winter.

These westernmost Algonquian-speakers of the Northeast were able to hunt other animals as well, including minks, otters, wolves, wolverines, beavers, and rabbits. These tribes supplemented their diet with wild foods gathered from the

## FIREFLY SONG (OJIBWA)

Flitting white-fire insects!
Wandering small-fire beasts!
Wave little stars about my bed!
Weave little stars into my sleep!
Come, little dancing white-fire bug,
Come, little flitting white-fire beast!
Light me with your white-flame magic,
Your little star-torch.

surrounding woods. The Sauk, Fox, and Miami peoples hunted buffalo and practiced some agriculture as well.

By late March the Ojibwa left their winter camps and headed for their summertime villages. On the way they joined other families in groves of sugar maples at rivers and lakes where fish were plentiful. This was a joyous time of reunion, for each year they returned to the same place rich with memories of maple-sugar making, a shared celebration that marked the end of winter's cold and isolation.

*Algonquian and Tete de Bule Indians show the interior of a birch-bark canoe, 1959. Such canoes were so maneuverable that French fur trader Samuel de Champlain encouraged his men to replace their clumsy French skiffs with birch-bark canoes.*

Some Algonquians were able to plant corn, squash, and tobacco in fields near their summer villages. However, because many lived farther north and had a shorter growing season, they could not rely on corn as could the Iroquois. Groups such as the Ojibwa of Minnesota and the Menominee of Wisconsin depended on wild rice to survive in areas of limited food resources. Wild rice is a seed-bearing grass that grows naturally along the muddy shores of marshes and streams, and these peoples divided the rice beds into units that individual families were allowed to harvest.

Summer was a reward for surviving the bitter winter. The Ojibwa and Menominee picked berries, told stories, played games, and visited with each other in between tanning hides and building canoes. The warm months made this an especially pleasant time for celebration ceremonies and puberty rites.

In the late spring or early fall, they celebrated the rituals of the Midewiwin, the Great Medicine Society, a secret society of healers founded in the early 1600s. Many of the Great Lakes Algonquian groups—the Ojibwa, Potawatomi, Menominee, Winnebago, Sauk, Fox, and Kickapoo—practiced the Midewiwin. Although there were some differences in the practices from tribe to tribe, they shared the same basic principles and purposes: to ward off disease and to prolong life.

Membership in the Great Medicine Society was not easily achieved. An apprentice had to show his dedication by devoting much time and concentration to learning herbal cures and rituals to invoke supernatural healing power. Then he underwent an initiation in the Midewiwin lodge that lasted several days. The climax of this ceremony came when he knelt in front of a Mide officer who seemingly injected the novice with cowrie shells. The novice then keeled over, appearing to die. Suddenly, the new member would recover, coughing up the cowrie shells that had supposedly entered his body. Through this initiation ceremony, the novice gained supernatural powers enabling him to heal himself and others.

Other important rites were solitary, such as the vision quest. When a boy reached puberty, his father took him to the woods where they constructed a rough shelter. His father returned to camp, leaving the boy alone to call out to the Creator for a personal vision that would link him more fully to the natural world and leave him with more understanding of his life. For four days and nights, his body growing weaker from lack of food and water, he waited alone, often frightened, for the appearance of his guardian spirit, which could come in the form of an animal or a human. Each morning the sun rose regardless of his state of mind, a silent reminder of his oneness with all life. Finally, his guardian spirit appeared to him with a special symbolic message from the spirit world, a message that would sustain him for the rest of his life and keep him on the right path, connected spiritually to all other forms of life.

Girls could also have guardian spirits, although this was not considered as necessary as it was for young men, who did most of the hunting and fighting. When girls reached puberty, they performed a similar rite outside the village, in which they fasted and waited to meet their guardian spirit.

## HOW THE MIDEWIWIN CEREMONY CAME TO THE PEOPLE

This is an account of the Miami people that tells of how the animals brought the ceremony to the people: We saw you very much afflicted, and were disposed to relieve your troubles. The power which has been given you, and the ceremonies which you have seen...men will [try to use] for purposes equally vicious and [honorable]. We enjoin it upon you to keep [this valuable profession] secret from the world....Conduct every part of the ceremony with gravity and secrecy and suffer no one to condemn it or ridicule its proceedings.

# >> EUROPEAN CONTACT <<

The European traders and settlers began settling the Atlantic coast of North America in the first half of the seventeenth century for many different reasons. In what is now Quebec, the French had come seeking gold and other precious metals; instead, they made their fortunes from the trade in fish and furs. Settlers followed, and from Massachusetts to the Carolinas, the English, Dutch, and Swedes came to the new land in search of religious freedom, economic opportunities, or wealth from the mining of precious metals. Unlike the fur traders, who wanted to maintain the wilderness with its rich supply of fur-bearing animals, the settlers wanted Indian land.

## THE PILGRIMS

*The Pilgrims receive the Wampanoag Indian Massasoit and his people. It was Massasoit who taught the Pilgrims how to cultivate corn. This skill, along with generous gifts of food from the Algonquian peoples, saved the Pilgrims from certain starvation.*

Unlike the Jamestown settlers, who were motivated by a desire to improve their economic standing, the Pilgrims landed in Massachusetts Bay in 1620 intent on achieving goals of a religious nature. Cast out of their own country because of their religious beliefs, the Pilgrims settled away from the colony of Virginia, which practiced the state religion of the Church of England. Dutch and Swedish settlers provided a buffer zone between these two groups.

By the time the Pilgrims arrived, disease had already greatly reduced the native population. The Pilgrims explained this wave of death as a gift from God; in their eyes, God had killed the natives to provide land for his chosen people. This kind of thinking led the Pilgrims to call the Pequot Indians children of Satan. At first, they tried to "save" the Indians by imposing their religion and their way of life on them. The Pilgrims thought that the natives' seasonal migrations were simply aimless and chaotic wanderings. Unable to understand the alternating schemes of hunting and gathering and fishing and farming that the Pequot had developed over the centuries, the Pilgrims attempted to turn them into settled farmers. When the Pequot resisted the Pilgrims' efforts to force them to live in cramped and unhealthy houses year round, the Pilgrims saw it as their divine mission to massacre the Pequots by the hundreds in 1637 by burning the fort where the Pequots had taken refuge.

# POCAHONTAS

*Pocahontas with her son.*

Pocahontas (1595–1617) is probably the most famous Indian woman. According to John Smith, a leader of the Jamestown colony, when her father, Chief Powhatan (1550–1618), captured and tried to execute him in 1607, Pocahontas interceded, saving Smith's life. Later, Pocahontas came to the fort with other Indians on diplomatic missions for her father. Pocahontas means "mischievous" and she probably earned her nickname as her powerful father's indulged favorite child.

White settlers and Indians continued to raid each other's camps until the English captured Pocahontas in April 1613. During her year-long captivity at Jamestown, she learned English manners and religion from a twenty-eight-year-old English widower named John Rolfe. They fell in love and decided to marry. The leader of the Jamestown colony and Powhatan hoped that such a marriage would seal a peaceful alliance. In June 1616, Pocahontas, her husband, their son, and a dozen Indian people arrived in England, where they met British royalty. However, Pocahontas died of tuberculosis in March 1617, before she could return to her homeland.

Both Indians and whites benefited from their first contact. The Europeans gave the Indians sharp knives, ax heads, muskets, and fishhooks that helped them to hunt, fish, gather food, and work wood and metal more easily. The Indians helped the newcomers survive their first years in what seemed to them a harsh and dangerous new land.

Many colonists came to America without hunting skills because hunting was a sport reserved for the upper classes in Europe. Commoners and peasants were punished for poaching if they tried to hunt. Largely city dwellers, many colonists were even afraid of the forests. They knew nothing of such strange animals as the antelope, moose, caribou, bison, alligator, turkey, and opossum.

The Algonquians of the Atlantic seaboard saved the new settlers from starvation. Massasoit, a Wampanoag Indian, taught the Pilgrims how to cultivate corn, which was a plant unfamiliar to

them but one well suited to North American soil. Similarly, the first permanent British settlement in the New World, at Jamestown, Virginia, survived its first winter (1607–1608) with the help of the Powhatans. The Indians not only taught the newcomers how to move silently through the forest in search of game, but they also showed them what nuts and berries were edible. The colonists learned from the Indians how to make canoes, snowshoes, buckskin clothing, and waterproof ponchos.

Soon after first contact, however, the Indians began to die in large numbers. Europeans were carriers of many illnesses, including measles, smallpox, typhus, tuberculosis, chicken pox, cholera, and influenza, from which the Indians had no natural immunities.

Their different ideas about land soon created conflicts between the Indians and the settlers. The whites wanted land that they could fence, plow,

## CAPTURED BY THE INDIANS

*A male relative tries to protect settler Jane Wells from her Indian captor. Images such as this often served to justify white hostility toward Indians and the taking of their lands.*

Benjamin Franklin once pointed out that:

When white persons of either sex have been taken prisoners young by the Indians, and have lived a while among them, tho' ransomed by their Friends, and treated with all imaginable tenderness to prevail with them to stay among the English, yet in a Short time they become disgusted with our manner of life...and take the first good Opportunity of escaping again into the Woods, from whence there is no reclaiming them.

An English settler named Frances Slocum was captured by the Delaware Indians in Pennsylvania in 1778 when she was a child. Sixty years later, her two surviving brothers discovered her whereabouts and traveled to the Indiana Territory to bring her home. Frances was now known as Ma-con-a-quah and refused to go with them, saying,

I have always lived with the Indians; they have always used me very kindly; I am used to them. The Great Spirit has allowed me to live with them; and I wish to live and die with them. Your wah-puh-mone [looking glass] may be larger than mine, but this is my home. I do not want to live any better, or anywhere else, and I think the Great Spirit has permitted me to live so long because I have always lived with the Indians.

Mary Jemison was captured by a French and Indian raiding party when she was a teenager in 1758. They brutally murdered her family and then gave Mary to two Seneca sisters. To the sisters, she was a long-lost child who replaced their slain brother. Mary lost all desire to return to the white way of life; she married and had children in the Seneca tribe. In her account of her life as told to a New York doctor in 1814, she described the Iroquois as varied and complicated human beings who lived by their own cultural logic.

and own for a lifetime and then pass on to their children. The Indians did not understand the idea of private land ownership but soon learned that they had to give up their land to the superior technology of the Europeans or be killed.

Sometime after 1614, the Englishman John Rolfe introduced Orinoco tobacco to the colony. The Virginia colonists seized upon this crop as the way to make their fortunes; within a century, the profitable sales of tobacco created the large, prosperous brick buildings of Williamsburg. But large-scale tobacco farming required huge tracts of land because this crop wore out the soil. Rather than clearing heavily wooded land, the colonists seized the fields the Indians had already cleared, pushing the Indians farther inland. The greedy colonists allowed their buildings and palisades to fall into ruin as they planted even their streets with tobacco.

The Powhatans had always treated the English considerately: they had welcomed them, had brought them food, and had taught them how to provide for themselves. Ambitious in a way the Indians never were, however, the English always demanded more. By 1622, they had taken all the banks of the James River and the mouths of its tributaries, pushing the Indians even farther back

**The Buck's Wife, Wife of the Whale,** *1835, George Catlin's portrait of a Sauk and Fox woman.*

## INDIAN MILITARY TACTICS

Many of the tactics successfully used by the American soldiers in their fight against the British came partly from the Indians, who had taught the colonists how to fight a guerrilla war. The British had the largest empire in the world, with more soldiers and better weapons than the colonists. However, they also had a rigid and old-fashioned way of fighting battles: European soldiers had to line up in formation because of the loading difficulties and inaccuracies of their muskets. The colonists soon learned to fight the way the Indians did, using hunting techniques. They often sent out a few men to lure the enemy into pursuit so that a larger group could surround the enemy and attack them on every side.

After Charleston fell to the British in 1780, the southern American army seemed to be fighting a losing war. But Francis Marion, a plantation owner in Berkeley County, South Carolina, applied the lessons he had learned from the Cherokee and attacked the British in surprise raids from the swamps. Outnumbered by the British, the Swamp Fox (as Marion was known thereafter) and his men avoided full-scale battles and lived off the land, harassing their enemies with Indian-style tactics. In Vermont, Ethan Allen led his Green Mountain Boys using a similar strategy. In many ways, the United States owes its independence to the Indians, whose fighting methods made it possible for a small group of colonists to defeat the most powerful military organization in the world.

*Mary Frances, 78, enjoys her favorite briar pipe, while her son sits beside her. Both mother and son, Algonquian Indians from Maine, are known for their expert basketry.*

into the interior. Not only was the riverside land prime farmland, but it also formed the link between the Indians' important hunting and gathering territories inland and their food-gathering areas on the river. The foreigners who lived in the settlements that separated the Powhatans' territories did not trust the Indians to pass back and forth. The Indians soon had no access to the rivers that they had traveled so freely only years before.

Frustrated by the colonists' failure to even try to understand their culture and full of despair for their future, the Powhatans attacked in March 1622, killing 350 English in the area. Although the Powhatans could have annihilated the Jamestown settlement, they did not. Instead, they attempted to send the British a strong message that they had gone too far. They did this symbolically: by killing the settlers with their own tools, they were reminding the colonists not to work the land to death. To show them not to eat up the land, the Indians stuffed dirt in some mouths. And to make the point that still others deserved to choke to death on their unbridled appetites, the Powhatans stuffed bread in the mouths of the rudest, most demanding settlers.

Not surprisingly, these symbolic messages went unheeded by the settlers, who actually believed their presence to be a benefit to the Indians. Losing a fourth of their colonists did not make the English want to withdraw; instead it made them send home for greater numbers in the hopes of eradicating "so cursed a nation, ungrateful to all benefits."

As the number of colonists continued to grow, the native population diminished. As the settlers grabbed more Indian lands to raise more soil-depleting tobacco, they nevertheless demanded that the Indians raise extra food on their shrinking land base.

In an attempt to force the Indians to conform to European standards, the settlers arranged the Treaty of 1646, which stated that the Powhatan leader held his dominions as a vassal of the king of England, which meant that he was responsible for supplying an annual tribute of twenty beaver skins and could not dispose of his lands at will, and that the English could even choose his successor. This marked a turning point for the Indians, who no longer had any chance of holding back the English. From then on, there were simply too many whites who were too determined to make their fortunes raising tobacco. When the first group of colonists had arrived in 1607, there had been almost 14,000 Powhatans; by 1669 there were 30,000 English and only about 2,900 Powhatans in Virginia's coastal plain. Later, the white government established small reservations for the remaining Powhatan people. Although these original reservations are much smaller today, the Powhatans are still very much there, living in the remnants of their native land.

Farther north, the European fur trade was creating drastic changes in native life. By the end of the 1500s, European demand for furs was so strong, and the payments so enticing, that among the Indians trapping for furs became more important than the traditional round of hunting, gathering, and farming. Men hunted, trapped, and processed the furs while women cleaned and tanned them. Many tribes were unintentionally uprooted in the quest for furs: the Ojibwa and some Iroquois moved farther west. As the Indians relied more upon flour, sugar, and other foods that their furs purchased, the

## THE FUR TRADE

New York City owes its identity as an important commercial center to its location and its early trade in Indian furs. John Jacob Astor (1763–1848), a butcher's son, became the richest man in North America by buying and selling furs through the American Fur Company.

The North American fur industry depended on Indian trappers and hunters who could use their skills and understanding of animal behavior to capture fur-bearing animals. Small groups of Indian men trapped the animals and took them back to a base camp, where Indian women processed their skins. Winter was the primary season for trapping because the animals grew their thickest furs then. Indians had developed snowshoes to travel across the surface of the snow and toboggans to transport large loads of cargo. They also developed deadfall traps: when a mink, ermine, marten, or otter tried to get the meat in the trap, the movement pulled a peg attached to the meat, which then released a log that crushed the animal. Trappers also snared animals with rawhide loops that choked the creatures when they unknowingly passed through the loops. Between 1534, when the first traders arrived, and 1850, when rubber and umbrellas began to replace rainproof beaver hats, the fur trade financed the building of cities such as New York, Montreal, Detroit, and Chicago. The growth of many of the great cities in the United States and Canada came out of the millions of beaver pelts, sealskins, moose hides, deerskins, bison hides, and otter pelts trapped by the Indians.

old ways of farming and following plants and animals in seasonal migrations began to disappear. Men spent their time hunting for furs instead of meat, and their families moved closer to trading posts for their own protection. As a result, native peoples became increasingly dependent upon European goods.

The fur traders also brought rum and whiskey to the Indians, who had no experience of alcohol. Unscrupulous white leaders even used liquor to secure chiefs' signatures or marks.

*This Ojibwa skin pouch features quill-work decoration; beads later replaced bird quills for decoration.*

While the fur trade was rapidly destroying centuries-old native ways of life, the Jesuits and other Christian missionaries were working devotedly to destroy native spiritual customs. The Jesuits arrived in 1612; unable to understand the Indians' spirituality and appalled by their way of life, these missionaries attempted to settle migratory peoples such as the Montagnais (an Iroquoian-speaking people) into permanent settlements. Unfortunately, such a concentration of people left the Indians open to disease, which quickly killed many and reduced their population.

The Huron, who already lived in more settled communities, responded to the Jesuit mission with openness to their religious message. The Huron had developed a profound set of philosophical ethics and powerful and deep-seated beliefs based on a supreme female deity. They believed that other gods helped this supreme deity to sustain all forms of life. The Huron also believed that everyone's soul had two sides and that the goal of life was to balance and integrate these two natures within each person. They held a deep-seated conviction that everyone was entitled to his or her own religious beliefs. Encouraged, the Jesuits failed to realize that the Huron response came from a sense of tolerance. Instead, the priests convinced themselves that the Indians practiced a pagan form of worship based on simplistic spiritual beliefs.

In addition to disrupting traditional Indian lifestyles and spiritual practices, the Europeans also disturbed the traditional balance of relationships among the tribes by only distributing weapons to some groups, in exchange for furs. In 1609, the French gave the Algonquians muskets, which they could use against the Mohawk. Later, the French also supplied the Huron with guns.

In 1615 the fur trader Samuel de Champlain joined the Huron on a failed raid against the Oneida (an Iroquois nation). He enjoyed close contact with the Indians because he did not assume that all European technology was superior; he admired Indian ingenuity. He also showed a surprising tolerance for native religion, in contrast to the Jesuits. Despite the failure of the raid, the Huron appreciated his presence. When the Oneida shot the Frenchman with an arrow, the Huron nursed him back to health in their home village during that winter.

By the 1640s, the Five Iroquois Nations, who were the traditional enemies of the Algonquians and the Huron, formed an alliance with the Dutch, who supplied them with guns. In 1649, the Five Nations slaughtered most of the 30,000 members of the Huron nation, giving the Iroquois control of the fur trade. However, for all the Huron they killed, they adopted hundreds more. Each captive joined a longhouse and a clan and became a full member of the community. This ability to integrate outsiders into their nations kept the Iroquois strong both in numbers and in tradition.

Along the Atlantic Coast, whites continued to push the Indians farther inland. In New England the Wampanoag chief, King Philip, led an alliance of his tribe and the Narranganset against the 50,000 white settlers, but was defeated in 1676. Although the western Great Lakes Indians did not feel white pressure until the 1780s, they, too, had to make room for the Eastern tribes and were pushed westward.

When four of the six tribes of the Iroquois Nation fought on the side of the British in the American Revolution, George Washington sent an army to destroy forty Iroquois villages and most of their crops. With American independence, settlers also pushed these groups farther west, into the homeland of the Algonquian Miami, Ottawa, Menominee, Ojibwa, Illinois, Potawatomi, Sauk, Fox, and the Siouan Winnebago.

The Indians never understood the white idea of land ownership; although the new American government would arrange treaties that transferred title to the Indians' lands to the United States, the Indians rarely comprehended what this meant. Furthermore, the Indian men the whites chose to call chiefs were seldom true leaders in their tribes. Nevertheless, if the Indians resisted moving off their lands, the U.S. Army freely used force. By 1855, the government had either moved all the Northeastern tribes to Western territories or restricted them to small reservations within their homelands.

## OREN LYONS, CONTEMPORARY LEADER

*Onondaga chief Oren Lyons.*

Oren Lyons, a present-day Onondaga chief, left his successful career as a commercial artist in New York City to return to his people as Faith Keeper of the Turtle Clan in the Iroquois Confederation. He was continuing a long tradition of faith keepers begun centuries before the Pilgrims landed at Plymouth Rock. In this role, he is charged with preserving and transmitting the memories and traditions of his people, based on the principles of democracy, community, and reverence for nature.

Upon accepting the role of Faith Keeper, Lyons noted, "Your first reaction is that you don't want to do that [assume so much responsibility] because the chiefs are always busy:...They're never home....The only words [my clan mother] said to me were 'Think of what you can do for your people....'"

Today this responsibility also includes speaking before the United Nations. When Lyons, other members of the Iroquois League, and a delegation of Lakota Indians addressed this organization in Geneva, Switzerland, they spoke up for the rights of the natural world, saying, "Where is the seat for the buffalo or the eagle? Who is representing them here in this forum? Who is speaking for the waters of the earth? Who is speaking for the trees and the forests?"

Oren Lyons also edits a publication called *Daybreak*, which is dedicated to the seventh generation unborn. When a chief is given instructions as he assumes his office in the League of the Iroquois, he is told that he sits in council for the welfare of the people in the seventh generation to come. Leaders are charged with the responsibility to make decisions that will ensure the survival of the world that we enjoy for seven generations after us. As Lyons said, "You suffer in direct ratio to your transgressions against the natural world....We are literally a part of nature." Personifying nature as a member of your family, rather than as something to be dominated, lies at the heart of the Native American way of thinking about life.

# CHAPTER TWO

# >THE<
# SOUTHEAST

*We desire to recall a little history of our people...the Choctaw and Chickasaw....The Government of the United States urged us to relinquish our valuable possessions there [east of the Mississippi River] to make homes for their own people and to accept new reservations west of the great river Mississippi, assuring us that there we would be secure from the invasion of the white man....We consented, and with heavy hearts we turned our backs upon the graves of our fathers and took up the dismal march for our new western home....After long...marches, after...much loss of life, we reached our new reservation.*

*In 1855...we sold the entire west part of our reservation...over 12 million acres....In 1866...we gave up all that part leased for the occupancy of friendly Indians....And again, in 1890 and 1891, we relinquished...3 million acres....Now in less than five years we are asked to surrender completely our tribal governments and...to allot our lands in severalty....*

—Delegates of the Choctaw and Chickasaw Nation
in their 1895 response to the Dawes Commission Report

# LANGUAGES OF THE TRIBES OF THE SOUTHEAST

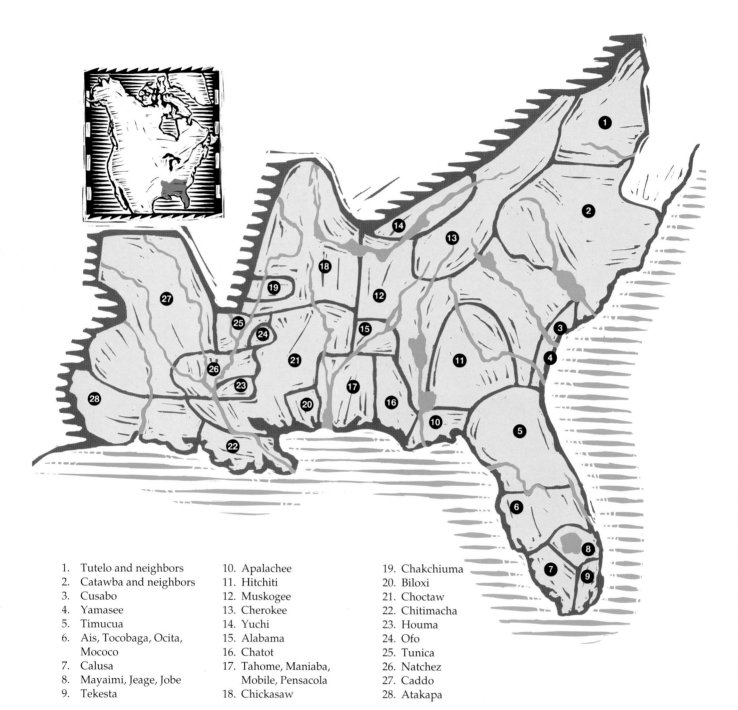

1.  Tutelo and neighbors
2.  Catawba and neighbors
3.  Cusabo
4.  Yamasee
5.  Timucua
6.  Ais, Tocobaga, Ocita, Mococo
7.  Calusa
8.  Mayaimi, Jeage, Jobe
9.  Tekesta
10. Apalachee
11. Hitchiti
12. Muskogee
13. Cherokee
14. Yuchi
15. Alabama
16. Chatot
17. Tahome, Maniaba, Mobile, Pensacola
18. Chickasaw
19. Chakchiuma
20. Biloxi
21. Choctaw
22. Chitimacha
23. Houma
24. Ofo
25. Tunica
26. Natchez
27. Caddo
28. Atakapa

*Many language families were represented in this region, including the Gulf tribes, who lived in Louisiana, Mississippi, Alabama, Florida, and Georgia. The Gulf tribes include the Muskogean-speakers such as the Choctaw, Chickasaw, Creek, Natchez, and Seminole, and the Caddoan-speakers such as the Caddo of northwest Louisiana. The Catawba and Yuchi of the Carolinas spoke a Siouan language, while their Cherokee and Tuscarora neighbors spoke an Iroquoian language.*

The Indians who inhabited America's Southeast, the warm, fertile coastal plains bordering the Atlantic and the Gulf of Mexico, had developed the most complex Indian societies north of Mexico. They built enormous earthen temple mounds, practiced agriculture, developed natural healing and curing medicines, produced elaborate ceremonial art, and built populous towns, basically urban centers that were almost organized into true states.

They also endured the relentless push of white settlers hungry for land from the mid-sixteenth century on. These native peoples were continually pushed farther and farther west as described by the Choctaw and Chickasaw in the preceding passage. The Dawes Commission, which they were addressing, had been established by the United States government in 1893 to further the integration of Indians into the larger white society. The members of this commission hoped that the division of Indian lands into individual plots would teach Indians the concept of individual rather than tribal land ownership. The Dawes Commission also proposed to open tribal lands to white settlement. In response to the Choctaw-Chickasaw plea, the commission recommended that the tribal governments of both nations be disbanded, a territorial government established, and their tribal lands allotted to individuals. The rest of the land would then be available for white settlers.

It is easy to understand why white settlers found this land of great natural abundance to be so attractive. Rivers and streams provided fish, while the forests were rich in game, edible plants, nuts, berries, and grasses. The Indians of this region enjoyed a more temperate climate than their northern relatives and could rely on farming for more of their food because of the longer growing season. The Natchez people were typical of the Southeastern tribes.

*Top: A Seminole father and his sons, near Miami, Florida. Above: Louis S. Glanzman's painting of a Hopewell Indian burial ceremony.*

# THE NATCHEZ

The Natchez, who gave their name to the modern-day Mississippi city near their homeland, had a highly developed culture with a complex form of government. Farming had freed them of the necessity to search for food, allowing them the time to develop a more sophisticated society. The Natchez shared many traits of the powerful Mississippian culture that had preceded them: their communities had temples for worship, elaborate ceremonial centers, large plazas, burial mounds, and dwellings.

By the time Europeans began to explore North America's Southeast, Natchez culture had already existed for at least five centuries, with the tribes living in stable, sophisticated societies. At this time, the Natchez lived in nine villages along a tributary of the Mississippi River. At the height of their civilization, there may have been as many as 4,500 Natchez, with an average population of 400 people per village.

Natchez society was organized into four classes, with commoners at the lowest level. Above the commoners, in ascending order, were the Honored Men, the Nobles, and the ruling class, the Suns. The most powerful member of Natchez society was the Great Sun. Considered to be a living god, the Great Sun had absolute power over his people. He lived on the highest pyramidal mound in the tribe's major village. From his residence, the Great Sun could see the temple, which crowned a tall mound on the other side of the open plaza. Chambers within the temple held an eternal fire, which was considered to be a gift of the sun, and the bodily remains of the current Great Sun's immediate predecessor.

In 1662, the Natchez first encountered Europeans when French settlers moved into the area. Contact with foreign disease and warfare with the French soon decimated the Natchez population. Finally, in 1731, the French destroyed the remaining Natchez villages, selling the rest of the people, including the Great Sun, into Caribbean slavery. The few Natchez who survived escaped to join nearby tribes, including the Chickasaw and the Creek.

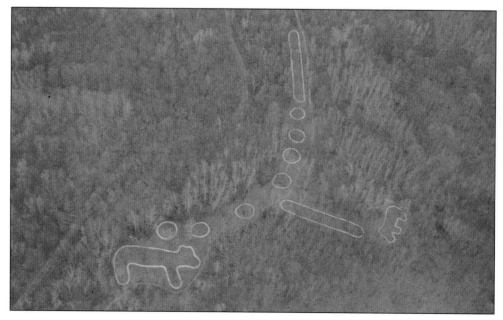

*Top: Obsidian blades and spear point from the Mound City Group National Monument, Iowa. Left: Estimated to be approximately 1,400 years old, the Great Bear Mound, located near Marquette, Iowa, is one of many elaborate effigy mounds created by early Native American cultures.*

# THE CREEK

The Creek lived mainly in what is now Alabama, although some groups had moved as far north as Georgia. They took their name from that of a river where an earlier band had once settled. Migration legends tell how various groups—the Muskogee, the Alabama, the Koasati, the Tuskegee, and the Hitchiti—came together to form the Creek Confederacy. By the early 1800s the Creek Confederacy consisted of nearly 22,000 people, which included about 18,000 Muskogee.

The Creek lived in pal-isaded towns. Each town had an open area or plaza at its center that included a winter council house 25 feet (7.6m) high, made of wood and bark and plastered with clay. This large, circular meeting house also pro-vided shelter for the aged

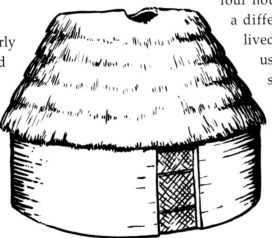

*A winter council house with a thatch roof.*

and the homeless. In sunny weather, tribal elders met outside, beneath the shade of the thatched roofs. The ceremonial center also included a field where participants played the ancient game of chunkey. In this game, a man and his teammate ran after a rimmed stone disk that the first man had

rolled, throwing wooden poles where they expected the disk to fall over.

Each family had between one and four rectan-gular houses made of wood and plaster with a shingled or cypress bark roof. Each house had a central fireplace.

When a family was wealthy enough to have four houses, each structure served a different purpose. The family lived in one during the winter, using it also as a kitchen. The second was a summer home and guest house. The third house was used to store grain and to provide shade in the hot summers, while the final building was used for the storage of raw materials such as skins and furs. Outside their homes, the Creek kept dogs and birds as pets.

Within the Creek chiefdom, people were orga-nized by clans named for animals. The following Creek legend explains how clans came into being:

When the Creek Indians looked back on their history, they found that for many generations they had been completely covered in a dense, blinding

## HERBAL MEDICINES

Nearly 200 Native American herbal treatments have been recognized as modern medicines. For example, the Indians commonly used willow to bring down fever; willow bark contains salicylic acid, the effective ingredient in aspirin. When they needed more energy, they added caffeine to their drinks long before cola drinks were invented. They may have also used digitalis, from the plant foxglove, to treat heart conditions.

By studying and experimenting with local plants, North American Indians developed a wide array of effective herbal medicines. The Indians of the Southwest used agave leaves as a tonic to prevent scurvy and a tea from the green bark of the oak to cure diarrhea. They also pounded and mixed animal fat with cattail roots for an effective burn salve. The White Mountain Apaches used the juice of walnut hulls to clean maggots from wounds and to rid horses and cattle of lice and other parasites. As modern medicine rediscovers the power of healing plants, scientists have begun to recognize the value of the powerful natural medicines that Indians have been using for centuries.

# LACROSSE

The tribes of the Eastern woodlands enjoyed many competitive team sports. One of the fiercest was stickball, which the French named "lacrosse" because the rackets resembled a bishop's crosier. Lacrosse as we know it today developed from the Iroquois form of the game, which uses a single racket or stick. The tribes of the Southeast used two rackets. These were made on a frame strung with hemp or squirrel skin. A ball was made from tightly packed deerskin.

Today's game of lacrosse is considerably tamer than its original form. The original stickball was such a violent game that it was considered a peacetime substitute for war. Almost any strategy was considered acceptable, including biting, stomping, and butting. Broken bones, torn ligaments, and even death were accepted as part of the game.

The painting above, by American artist George Catlin (1796–1872), depicts the Choctaw version of lacrosse in which warriors and nobles wore egret feather costumes and the insignia of their towns and clans. Catlin also wrote of the game, in which some seven hundred players tried to catch the ball in their sticks and throw it to their goal. The players ran, leaped over each other's heads, and darted between each other's legs, tripping each other and screaming in high "shrill yelps and barks! Every mode is used that can be devised to oppose the progress of the foremost who is likely to get possession of the ball; and these obstructions often meet desperate resistance, which terminate in violent scuffles and sometimes in fisticuffs...."

Games were played between the residents of towns of neighboring tribes. Major social events, the games often drew more than a thousand spectators, including bettors who waged furs and skins on the outcome. To initiate a match, a team sent formal invitations to the opposing team in the form of painted sticks. By touching the invitation stick, a player accepted the challenge. The playing field, which measured about 230 feet (70.1m) in length, was then carefully prepared.

Then, as today, ball games were enjoyed as physical sports that were mentally challenging. The games also had a more profound spiritual and social significance. The ball game was an important part of the yearly ritual cycle designed to restore and maintain order in the universe and ensure humanity's continued well-being for the coming year. As elements of the great annual festivals, the ball games required of their participants a sense of awe and religious behavior that included fasting and the drinking of sacred medicine. Medicine men offered prayers. The game drew people together and brought them a sense of pride in belonging to their particular clan, village, and tribe.

fog. Because they could not see, they were dependent on their other senses, especially that of touch, in their efforts to find food. As they searched for food, the people became separated into groups. Each group was careful to stay within calling distance of the other groups. At last a wind arose from the east, gradually driving the fog from the land. As the fog lifted, the first group of people who were able to see the land and the various objects of nature took the name Wind clan. The first things seen by the Wind clan were a skunk and a rabbit, which had accompanied them through the fog. Although they did not adopt either of these animals as their clan symbol, they did declare them their closest friends and took on the duty of always protecting and defending these animals from physical injury and ridicule. Other groups of people came to light as the fog continued to disappear before the driving east wind, and each group adopted as its clan symbol the first animal the people saw, the animal that had traveled through the fog with them.

The Creek divided their twelve-month year into two seasons: winter and summer. Winter, which began with the Green Corn ceremony in the month of Much Heat (August), also included Little Chestnut (September), Big Chestnut (October), Frost (November), Big Winter (December), and Little Winter (January). The months of summer were Wind (February), Little Spring (March), Big Spring (April), Mulberry (May), Blackberry (June), and Little Heat (July).

The peoples of the Southeast celebrated many rituals to mark the passage of the months and the seasons. Their most important festival was the Green Corn ceremony, also known as the Busk, which they celebrated when the autumn corn ripened in August. This festival of renewal—an occasion when all crimes except murder were formally forgiven—marked the beginning of the new year. It was also a time of giving thanks for a successful harvest.

When the Busk began, the women scrubbed every part of their houses and all their cooking utensils and extinguished their hearth fires. At the

*Mistippee, a Creek Indian, dressed in the European-inspired dress of the Southeast. His bandolier bag (a bag worn over one shoulder and across the body) is decorated with beadwork.*

same time, the men repaired the council house and other communal buildings. During this period, men and women were not allowed to have any contact. To purify themselves, the people fasted on the second day before feasting on the third day. On the fourth and most important day, the high priest relit the sacred fire in the council house, using a ceremonial fire drill to spark flames that kindled the fire logs to which four ears of new corn had been added. He used the wing feathers of a white swan to fan the flame into a blazing fire. Elders circled the sacred fire in the Green Corn Dance while the members of the village watched. Later, the women took coals home from the sacred fire to relight the fires in their own dwellings. Then they prepared feasts on their newly lit fires. To purify themselves for the new year, everyone bathed together in a stream near the village.

The Creek traveled farther in search of food than did the Natchez, possibly because there had been a greater abundance of game near the Natchez

*Cherokee Sampson Boss Welch demonstrates the use of a cane blowgun and poison dart. The Cherokee used blowguns to hunt squirrels, rabbits, and birds.*

and by drinking a special herbal mixture before he set off to hunt. Hunting was a ritual activity, which always included prayers to the animals who gave up their lives. A shaman who oversaw the prayers was part of every hunting group that participated in a drive. Deer and bear were the main targets of the hunters. Men and boys used rabbit clubs to kill rabbits, while traps and snares captured both animals and birds. The Creek also caught fish and turtles and their eggs for food. The Creek, as well as most of the tribes in the Southeast, used the blowgun to kill small animals and birds, and fish poison to drug the fish so that they could be easily gathered from the water's surface.

Upon their return from the hunt, they prepared their fields for planting and sowed their crops, including corn (three varieties), squashes, beans, sunflowers, pumpkins, and melons. The men and women of the town worked in a common field. The women also worked the small garden plot that belonged to each family, located near their house. In addition, the women gathered wild plants such as cane seed, wild rice, nuts, wild sweet potato, persimmon, and other fruits and berries.

villages. While the Natchez had hunted for only two months at most, the Creek left their villages for nearly half the year. Leaving the sick and the old alone in the village, they hunted from October at least until March. Entire families accompanied the men on hunting trips, camping in family groups. Each man purified himself through the sweat bath

Women did more than tend crops and prepare meals; they also made pottery, wove baskets and mats, tanned animal skins, and made shirts, breechclouts, leggings, and cloaks.

## THE GAME OF HOOP AND SPEAR

The hoop and spear game was even more popular than lacrosse; this game tested a player's fleetness, eyesight, and skill in spear throwing. The object was to stop a moving hoop by spearing it with a wooden pole. The Choctaw of the Southeast used a round stone disk instead of a hoop and called this game chungke, which meant "running hard labor."

Hoops could range in size from only a few inches to eighteen inches (45.7cm) in diameter. Some hoops were made of stone while others, made of pliable sticks, had elaborate rawhide networks woven on them. Spears could be small darts and arrows or poles up to fifteen feet (4.5m) long.

Although a small-scale version of this game could be played indoors, it was usually an outside game played on a smooth, level course about fifty yards (45.7m) long.

The hoop and spear game could be played by two players or by teams. When two played, one carried the hoop and both carried their spears as they ran side by side. Once the hoop hit the ground, both men tried to hurl their spears through it in an effort to stop the hoop as soon as possible. Points were scored on the basis of colored markings along the spear and along the rim of the hoop. The highest score came from stopping the hoop with the first six inches (15.2cm) from the point of the spear.

# ≫ EUROPEAN CONTACT ≪

When the Spanish explorer Juan Ponce de León arrived in Florida in 1513, his men destroyed the Indian villages they discovered, killing and enslaving the native peoples. Possibly more dangerous was that the Indians had no natural immunity to the many diseases the Europeans carried. Measles, smallpox, chicken pox, cholera, typhus, influenza, and tuberculosis swept through entire villages and Native Americans died by the thousands.

In 1539, Spain sent Hernando de Soto to Florida with orders to "conquer, pacify, and people" the land for Spain. Although de Soto left no permanent settlements, the Spaniards, English, and French who came after him did. All three colonial powers attempted to conquer and settle the Southeast for themselves. In their battles for dominance, they paid little attention to the fate of the Indians, who had lived there for centuries.

By the beginning of the eighteenth century, the Spanish controlled Florida. They sent missionaries to convert the Indians to Christianity and to force them to work in the fields, supplying

*John White's rendering of a Carolina Indian ceremony.*

the missions with food. Meanwhile, the British were expanding their colonies from their home base in Charleston, South Carolina, relying on trade to gain an economic stronghold over the Indians, who did not understand a system that allowed them to obtain goods on credit in exchange for the promise of deerskins. At the same time, the French established outposts along the lower Mississippi River, but they suffered from a shortage of settlers because few people were willing to emigrate from France.

The new European colonies required large numbers of slaves to clear the land and bring it into cultivation. The English and French soon followed the Spanish pattern of taking Indian captives as slaves, most of whom were sold to owners at distant destinations so that they could not find their way home. This inhumane practice not only provided field hands but also opened tribal homelands for white settlement.

In 1763, the French lost the French and Indian War to the British and relinquished their claims to North America. British colonists then pushed across the Appalachian Mountains to settle in western Georgia and the Carolinas. In 1793, Eli Whitney invented the cotton gin, making it much less time-consuming to extract the seeds from the blossom. As a result, farmers planted more acreage with cotton, a crop that quickly depleted the soil but had great profit potential. As had the tobacco growers farther north, the cotton planters needed new land. To get it, they pressured Indians to sign away their land in exchange for the cancellation of debts to white traders.

The United States gained its independence in 1776, after which land-hungry settlers began to force their state governments, starting with Georgia, South Carolina, Alabama, and Mississippi, to move the few remaining Indians from the lands they still held. At this time, whites vastly outnumbered the natives, who were living in small, isolated areas, which were

*Many whites were aware of the government's unjust and cruel treatment of the Cherokee. This 1883 political cartoon depicts the Cherokee Nation bound and exploited by white settlers, railroad magnates, oil tycoons, and the United States courts.*

## THE CHEROKEE STORY OF THE DOOR THROUGH THE SKY

Once seven young men decided to travel to the sun. Off they walked, but after many days and many adventures, when they reached the sunrise place at the end of the earth, they discovered that the sky was solid. They could not get through to visit the sun. As they stood there, wondering what to do, the sky vault lifted, making a kind of doorway to the other side. Perhaps they could slip under to find the sun and see what her home was like.

Just then the sun herself appeared in the doorway and began to climb the sky. She was very bright and cast off so much heat that the young men had to step back and cover their eyes. One of the men decided to try the doorway. He leaped forward just as the sky closed again with a crash, crushing him between the sky and the earth. The remaining six decided it was too risky to try their luck, and though they missed their friend, they turned back toward home. Somehow, the return took longer than the trip to the sun, and they were old men when they finally made it home again. They never did see the face of the sun.

all that remained of their ancestral lands. Many whites felt that they had a right to the land of the Indians, whom they called "uncivilized heathens."

Ironically, after almost two hundred years of interaction with whites, the major Indian nations of the Southeast were known among themselves as the Five Civilized Tribes (the Cherokee, Chickasaw, Choctaw, Creek, and Seminole). They had adapted to white culture to a greater degree than had the Indians of any other region: many of them had white blood and owned houses, farms, livestock, and even, like their white neighbors, slaves. They used sophisticated agricultural methods. A number of these Indians had even converted to Christianity.

When tensions between Britain and the United States escalated into the War of 1812, many Indians of the Southeast nations fought on the British side, hoping to regain their own independence from the Americans. The Shawnee warrior Tecumseh led these fights against American forces, and even after his death, the Indians fought on. In 1814 General Andrew Jackson retaliated, leading an army that, surprisingly, included many Indians. These Creek, Cherokee, and Choctaw warriors fought for Jackson against their own people in return for the promise of being allowed to remain in their homelands. Despite his promises, however, many of Jackson's

Indian soldiers were eventually forcibly removed to Oklahoma Indian Territory.

The War of 1812 ended with the Treaty of Ghent in 1814. With the European presence gone, the Indians were no longer able to balance tribal interests against European demands. From 1815 on, Native Americans had to deal with the Americans on American terms. Even more Creek refugees and runaway slaves joined their Seminole relatives, seeking shelter in Florida's swampy terrain. Angry planters who wanted their slaves back asked the federal government to intervene.

At the same time, state governments, seeking land for settlers, were attempting to force the remaining Cherokee, Creek, Choctaw, and Chickasaw to relinquish all claim to their ancestral lands and move far away. The Cherokee, who lived in North Carolina, led the most organized resistance to removal, using every legal effort to retain their land. Between 1789 and 1825, they made thirty treaties with the United States government, losing more of their homeland with each agreement.

Of all the Southeastern peoples, the Cherokee had become the most "civilized" by white standards. The great thinker Sequoyah had devised a syllabary—a set of written characters to record their language—and they had their

## SEQUOYAH

The famous Cherokee Sequoyah (1760–1843) is the only man in history known to have single-handedly devised a written language. He was convinced that literacy was the key to achieving the power of the whites. Working alone, Sequoyah created a syllabary for his people in the early nineteenth century. Hundreds of Cherokees had learned to read and write their language by the 1820s.

**The Earth Is Our Mother,** *a painting by Creek Indian Jimmie C. Fife, depicts leaders of the Choctaw, Creek (Muskogee), Seminole, Chickasaw, and Cherokee Nations.*

*The Trail of Tears. After the exodus, John Burnett, United States Army interpreter during the march, declared: "Murder is murder....Somebody must explain the four thousand silent graves that mark the trail of the Cherokees to their exile."*

own newspaper, tax-supported schools, and a written constitution with a legislature, code of laws, and a court system.

Although many whites joined in the fight for the Indians' right to retain what remained of their traditional lands, the state governments, responding to pressure from other settlers, nevertheless passed laws to take away not only the native peoples' lands but also their right to appear in court. This denial of fundamental Indian rights enraged then–Chief Justice of the Supreme Court, John Marshall, who declared it unconstitutional.

Despite three favorable decisions by Supreme Court Justice Marshall, in 1830 then-President Andrew Jackson signed the Indian Removal Act, forcing the Cherokee and a dozen other tribes to give up their ancestral lands and move to entirely strange country located west of the Mississippi.

Between 1830 and 1838, approximately 60,000 people, most of the members of the Five Civilized Tribes, journeyed west. Among these were some 11,500 Cherokees, who were forced to leave the wooded highlands of their homeland in the Great Smoky Mountains. Under military guard, they walked the 1,200-mile (1,920km) Trail of Tears to the so-called Indian Territory, located in present-day Oklahoma. To prevent any of the Indians from trying to run for the mountains, soldiers often brutally seized people from their houses at bayonet point, driving them outside as their homes were set on fire. Many had to leave their belongings behind. Children were separated from their parents, and husbands and wives never saw each other again. Along the journey, cold, rain, wind, and mud were constant companions until the winter snow came. At night, exhausted though they were, the Indians found sleep difficult under the soggy blankets. When sleet turned to wet snow, they wrapped strips of blankets around their feet in an effort to protect themselves from frostbite. Under these terrible conditions, cholera and measles spread like wildfire. As many as a quarter of the Cherokees may have died along the way. When they arrived in their new territory, the western tribes who lived there opposed this new intrusion, killing and plundering many of the newcomers.

During the period of removal, some members of the Five Civilized Tribes had managed to scatter and hide in their traditional lands. Some Choctaws sought refuge in the backwoods of Louisiana and Mississippi until the federal government finally established a reservation for them in east central Mississippi in the 1900s. Some Cherokees hid in the mountains of North Carolina, Tennessee, Georgia, and Alabama. Despite continued pressure for them to join the rest of their people in Oklahoma, this Eastern Band of Cherokee Indians stayed put until they finally acquired reservation land in the Southeast. The Creek scattered into the far reaches of their homeland, which included the greater portion of Alabama. The United States government finally acknowledged those who had remained with a tract of land in southern Alabama.

## ARTS AND CRAFTS OF THE SOUTHEAST

Some groups of the Southeast such as the Cherokee and Catawba still produce pottery and other items such as split baskets, wooden masks, and blowguns. The Chitimacha of Louisiana continue their tradition of making fine cane baskets.

The Seminole create unique and dramatic patchwork clothing by cutting and sewing tiny scraps of different-colored cloth into long strips of fabric. They then sew these long strips of geometric designs together into larger pieces to make skirts and jackets. By 1910, twenty years after the Seminoles first obtained sewing machines, this method of dressmaking had completely replaced the old appliqué method.

*Left: An 84-year-old Seminole patchworker. Above: A Choctaw basket weaver from Mississippi.*

# THE SEMINOLE

Although a few Seminoles went to Oklahoma on the Trail of Tears, most of them hid in the swampy undergrowth of the Florida Everglades. The Seminole were the only Indian nation formed as a direct result of European contact. Descended primarily from the once-powerful Creek nation, the Seminole people were an amalgam of many different southeastern tribes. In the early 1700s, British settlers from the Carolinas had invaded Florida, annihilating or impounding into slavery thousands of Florida Indians, and by the 1750s, the original Florida tribes had almost disappeared. Fleeing from the British, the Creeks from Georgia spread into Florida, absorbing what remained of the Florida tribes, other tribes from the Southeast, and escaped African slaves as well. This combination of peoples came to be known as the Seminoles, a name that translates as "Runaways," and refers to the fact that

they had broken away from the Creek nation. For a time the Seminole enjoyed relative peace under easygoing Spanish rule.

Over time, the Seminole developed a unique culture. Originally, their society was similar to that of the Creek: they were basically farmers, living in scattered camps with family-owned gardens where they grew crops such as corn, beans, melons, and tobacco. Many people kept horses and livestock. They caught fish in the Florida rivers. The abundant forests provided them with game such as deer, bear, and turkeys.

While some Seminoles lived in frame and log structures, others lived in chickees, which were open-sided homes measuring about 9 by 16 feet (2.7 by 4.8m) that were built atop platforms above the ground. These houses were ideally suited to the marshy ground and torrential rains typical of

*Seminole men prepare to cast off from shore in their cypress log dugout. For steering, they used both poles and paddles.*

*A Seminole chickee, with palmetto log supports and a thatch roof.*

that part of Florida. Palmetto trees provided the materials for the chickee: the basic structure was made of logs, while the steep roof was thatched with fronds. The pitch of the roof created a natural storage space in which articles remained dry and protected from the slanting rain that could enter the edges of the open platform. Today, many Seminoles still live in chickees.

The large number of African-Americans who lived among the Seminole was a constant source of conflict between the Indians and the slave owners. Although some slaves were runaways, many had been purchased by the Indians from white owners. The Seminole treated these people as equals rather than slaves, intermarrying with them and valuing their advice in council. Slavery was not a common Indian practice: of all the North American tribes, only the rank-conscious Mississippian and Northwest Coast peoples practiced a formal system of ownership and subjugation.

After the War of 1812, then-General Andrew Jackson relentlessly hunted down Seminoles when he led his army into northern Florida to round up runaway slaves. His troops burned and looted Seminole villages, and even captured Spanish cities in Florida—Jackson blamed the Spanish for having failed to control the Indians. After Spain ceded Florida to the United States in 1819, Jackson, the first

## BUFFALO JIM, CONTEMPORARY MEDICINE MAN

**B**uffalo Jim, an aged Seminole medicine man, lives on the Big Cypress Indian Reservation in southern Florida. The Big Cypress is basically a brown expanse of deep, dry grass broken only by knoll-like islands in a sea of sawgrass. This land is a natural drugstore of healing remedies.

When authors Harvey Arden and Steve Wall visited Buffalo Jim in his plain cinderblock house in 1989, he was one hundred years old. Buffalo Jim speaks only the Miccosukee language fluently, and he is greatly revered by his people for his spiritual powers and his knowledge of herbs. For more than seventy years, he has practiced natural medicine.

Stepping outside his modern house to a traditional open-air chickee thatched with palm, Buffalo Jim spoke of prophecy:

"The Creator told us two things will happen just before the end of the world. The first thing is that we will lose our language. That will be one of the signs. And already, you see, the children cannot speak the old language anymore. And the second sign is that we will forget how to make our sacred fire. No one really knows how to do it anymore. They may try, but they don't really know if they're doing it the right way, the way the Creator taught us long ago. I barely remember how the Old Ones did it. I was just a boy then in the 1890s."

Buffalo Jim also reflected on Coacoochee-Chief Wildcat—a medicine man who was captured with Osceola. Although Osceola died in prison, Wildcat escaped by doing magic. Buffalo Jim explained, "For four days he didn't eat anything. The soldiers laughed at him. They threw water at him. But on the fourth night he made the stone wall so soft that he reached his hands in like this and made a hole and let the people go through and he also squeezed the people small enough so they could go through that hole. Once they were out he told them to head south and he made it so the soldiers were like asleep and so the dogs couldn't bark and so the people made no tracks where their feet touched the ground. We had great leaders back then, leaders who could make a miracle, who knew the old Instructions."

*Below: War leader Osceola pictured in traditional Seminole dress. Left: William Osceola (who may be descended from the famous leader) teaches his children how to wrestle an alligator, a sport made famous by the Seminole.*

governor of the new American territory, continued his campaign against the Seminole. Armed posses of slave catchers hunted runaway blacks and Seminoles alike.

In 1823, the Seminole were given an inland reservation and promises of rations, livestock, and money for schools. However, the land was so poor that farming was virtually impossible; the Seminole there began to die of starvation. At the same time, the United States government withheld their rations in an attempt to recover former slaves from the Seminole population. The government refused to recognize that many blacks had been purchased and set free by the Seminole or were free because they had not been born into slavery. When Southern slave hunters invaded the reservation, hostilities escalated, and the Seminole struck back to protect their people. Warfare began in earnest when President Jackson signed the Indian Removal Act in 1830. The Seminole who remained in Florida fought a series of fierce

guerrilla battles against federal troops between 1835 and 1858 known as the Seminole Wars.

The Seminole's most famous leader, Osceola, was actually of Creek and white descent and was born in Georgia. A strong leader who was steadfast in his opposition to removal, by 1834 he had risen to a position of prestige among the Seminole. War continued to take its toll on both sides, leaving the Seminole exhausted from months of hiding and fighting. In 1837, Osceola was finally seized under a false white flag of truce. Despite a public outcry against such unfair tactics, he was taken to Fort Moultrie, South Carolina, where he died in prison early the following year. Other Seminole warriors carried on the fight.

The Seminole were gradually driven farther south into the Everglades until the government finally abandoned its struggle to deport them to Oklahoma. Today two Indian tribes are federally recognized in Florida: the Seminole and the Miccosukee. The latter are an offshoot of the original Seminole. During the years of persecution, they scattered and hid. Today they maintain more traditional ways of dress, language, religion, and life. In addition, the Poarch Band of Creeks own a small amount of land in extreme northwest Florida.

# THE INDIANS OF SOUTH CAROLINA

In some areas of the South the question of racial origins remains an extremely sensitive issue. In South Carolina, for example, the Indians (mainly Catawba) have been a third group in a white-black system and have often had to struggle to maintain their identity.

In addition to the Catawba, South Carolina's Indians include the Wateree, the Congaree, the Saraw (Cheraw), the Waccamaw, and the Saponi. The Catawba remain the major tribe in the state today. Federally recognized for the period from 1943 to 1962, they continue to be recognized by the state of South Carolina.

Other Indian communities in this state, however, have had a more difficult time because they have neither federal nor state recognition as Indian. These people live in clustered households, isolated from other Indians. Some of these small communities have tried to gain official federal and state recognition as Indian since the early 1970s. Three such groups—the Edisto, the Santee, and the Pee Dee—have created the Council of Native Americans of South Carolina. From the Greenville-Spartanburg area a group of urban Indians calling themselves the Piedmont Indians have joined the council, and the Catawba joined in 1988. Some groups maintain their Indian identity but do not belong to the council.

Because of the changing racial philosophy of South Carolina, the status of the Indians, who do not fit into the traditional racial categories, has also changed through time. The King of England granted the Catawba a reservation in 1763. During the colonial period, the Catawba were outside the racial system while the more assimilated Indians tended to be classified as "free persons of color," a category that included everyone who was neither white nor a slave. After 1792, free persons of color between the ages of sixteen and fifty were charged a capitation tax to maintain their freedom. If people could prove that their mothers were Indian, they were exempt from this tax. Thus, it was a great benefit to have someone testify to one's Indian ancestry. Many of the people who claimed to be Indian would now be considered white, while others would be thought of as black. Others did not file affidavits—which could have been as simple as a formal letter from someone who thought that a person's mother was of Indian ancestry—to prove their Native American descent. Indianness was hardly a distinct ethnic category.

After the Civil War the category of free persons of color disappeared, and more rigid racial divisions came into existence. When racial segregation ended, the Indians of South Carolina had to search for their ethnic ancestry. For the groups in South Carolina, Indian ancestry was determined by society and was open to negotiation. Thus, the concept of Indianness has actually changed through time.

*Catawba Indians Robert Lee Harris and his wife, Nettie Owl Harris in 1922.*

# CHAPTER THREE

# >THE<
# GREAT PLAINS

*From Wakan Tanka, the Great Spirit, there came a great unifying life force that flowed in and through all things—the flowers of the plains, blowing winds, rocks, trees, birds, animals—and was the same force that had been breathed into the first man....*

*Kinship with all creatures of the earth, sky, and water was a real and active principle....*

*This concept of life and its relations was humanizing, and gave to the Lakota an abiding love. It filled his being with the joy and mystery of living; it gave him reverence for all life; it made a place for all things in the scheme of existence with equal importance to all....*

— Chief Luther Standing Bear

Oglala Sioux (Central Plains) 1868–1939

# LANGUAGES OF THE TRIBES OF THE GREAT PLAINS

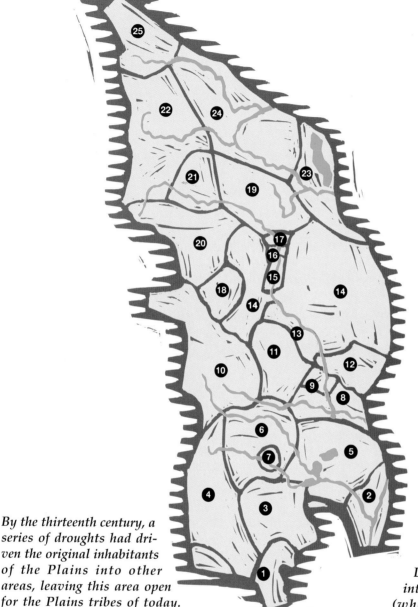

1. Tonkawa
2. Quapaw
3. Wichita and Kichai
4. Comanche
5. Osage
6. Kiowa
7. Kiowa-Apache
8. Missouri
9. Kansa and Oto
10. Arapaho
11. Pawnee
12. Iowa
13. Ponca and Omaha
14. Santee, Yankton, and Teton Sioux
15. Arikara
16. Mandan
17. Hidatsa
18. Cheyenne
19. Assiniboin
20. Crow
21. Gros Ventre
22. Blackfeet
23. Plains Ojibwa
24. Plains Cree
25. Sarcee

*By the thirteenth century, a series of droughts had driven the original inhabitants of the Plains into other areas, leaving this area open for the Plains tribes of today. Many factors brought these tribes to the Great Plains: drought in their former homelands, increasing population pressure, and later the arrival of white settlers who took Indian lands, forcing the Woodland tribes to move farther west.*

*The Caddoan-speaking Pawnee were probably the first to arrive, coming northward from east Texas into Nebraska about A.D. 1300. The Caddoan-speaking Wichita followed them.*

*By 1400, the Siouan speakers had moved west from the eastern prairies onto the Great Plains: the Mandan and the Assiniboines settled in what is*

*now North Dakota; the Crow and Hidatsa in Montana; the Ponca and the Sioux in South Dakota. The Sioux were separated into three main divisions: the Santee (who call themselves Dakota), the Yankton (who call themselves Nakota), and the Teton (whose name for themselves is Lakota). Each of the three divisions of the Sioux is further separated into groups; each group is broken down into separate bands.*

*At the same time, the Algonquian tribes moved from the east to areas even farther west than the Siouan speakers. This included the Plains Cree, who settled in what is now Saskatchewan; the Blackfeet and Gros Ventre, who came to Montana; and the Cheyenne and Arapaho, who settled in eastern Wyoming and Colorado.*

In the brief period—slightly more than a century—between acquiring the horse and losing their freedom, the Indians of the Great Plains were among the finest mounted warriors in history. Their nomadic lifestyle during the 1800s was also unique, a response to contact with the Europeans, who brought the horse to the New World.

Although prehistoric Plains hunters working in small nomadic bands had successfully hunted buffalo (different from the European buffalo and more correctly called bison), it was the horse that provided the Plains tribes with the mobility that allowed them to kill enough buffalo to sustain large groups of people. The legendary buffalo-hunting warriors of the Plains were actually relative newcomers to this region. The original inhabitants of the Plains had left the area by the 1200s because of drought.

About a century later, driven both by drought and by increased population in their homelands, groups from neighboring areas began to move into the region. Much later, pressure from white settlers was to push the Indians of the Northeast and Southeast westward into the same area. The Plains culture of the 1700s and 1800s actually consisted of two groups of people: the well-known nomadic tribes such as the Sioux and Cheyenne and the village-bound farmers such as the Mandan and Missouri Indians.

*Top: A Sioux woman with a board cradle on her back moves camp with her people; a travois is lashed to her horse. Above: While young boys practice with their bows and arrows, Sioux women prepare animal hides, letting the meat dry on racks beside their tipis.*

*In this 1832 painting, Mandan warriors dance the Bull Dance, part of a four-day Okipa ceremony.*
*The ceremony is held in the central plaza of the village, allowing spectators to watch atop the lodge roofs.*

# SETTLED VILLAGE FARMERS

The Mandan and Hidatsa were living in their villages along the Missouri River long before the white man brought the horse to their lands. Originally they had lived in the prairie lands along the Minnesota river, but by A.D. 1400, population pressure made them leave the Woodlands and move farther west, where they established large palisaded villages. They found the rich soil of the Mississippi Valley ideal for farming and quickly adapted themselves to Plains life, adding summer and autumn buffalo hunts to their routine of farming and gathering foodstuffs.

Each village, built on a rise, had a formal town plan featuring a central plaza—the gathering place for ceremonies and competitive games. There the men honed their skills as warriors and hunters, planned buffalo hunts in summer, and conducted religious ceremonies. One such ceremony was the Buffalo Calling Dance, in which dancers acted out a buffalo hunt: when a dancer tired and began to fall to the ground, another performer shot him with a blunt arrow; bystanders then pretended to skin the fallen dancer. The Buffalo Calling Dance could last for weeks—until a herd of buffalo was sighted.

Mandan and Hidatsa women maintained small garden plots in the rich riverbank lands to cultivate maize, beans, squashes, sunflowers, pumpkins, and tobacco. The soft soils of river bottoms were ideal for these people because their tools were not strong enough to break the tough sod of the prairie uplands. Undependable rainfall also made the prairies unsuitable for farming. In contrast, the river bottoms provided moist soil as well as protection from frost and scorching summer winds.

The farming people prospered in the Mississippi Valley, and they produced enough surplus to trade with other tribes. By 1750, the horse enabled the Mandan, Hidatsa, Arikara, and Pawnee peoples to extend the length of their bison hunt from a few weeks to months at a time, but instead of basing their entire way of life on the buffalo, they continued to return home to plant, harvest, and spend winter in the snug warmth of their earth lodges.

Farming was vitally important to groups such as the Mandans, who had very elaborate agricultural rituals. Not only did they pray for divine assistance in making their crops grow, but they also held annual agricultural ceremonies plus other rituals that could be performed when necessary.

An important element of these rituals was the sacred ceremonial bundle, which was a collection of items to be used in the ceremony. Bundles could include seeds of corn and other plants, rocks, pollen, minerals, and prayer sticks. The keeper of the bundle, who was the priest for all tribal rituals that used the bundle and the ceremonial equipment it contained, had a spiritual obligation to memorize and conduct the ceremony and to maintain the bundle. Bundles were considered to be alive, which meant that they had to be treated with respect. The bundle keeper also had to live an upstanding life, a life in harmony with nature. Sacred rites of inheritance determined who received the bundle; a person could use it only after years of study, which ensured the bundle's continued blessing upon the tribe. The Indians used the sacred bundle as part of tribal ceremonies of renewal and to overcome illness and hunger; a sacred bundle and its ceremonies were vital to the continued existence of the people.

In the spring, before planting time, the owner of the corn bundle washed the seeds so that they would germinate. He then called the spirits of the corn back from the south, asking them to help the crops grow. Finally, he distributed corn, bean, sunflower, and squash seeds to the women, who paid him with elk robes.

Like the eastern tribes, the Hidatsa celebrated the Green Corn Ceremony when the first corn of summer ripened. While shamans chanted, warriors hold-

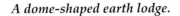

*A dome-shaped earth lodge.*

*Mandan women constructing a bull boat. These boats, used only by women, were made of rawhide stretched over willow frames.*

tanned hides, and even helped in the heavy construction of their compact earth lodges that clustered around the large central open area. As with the Iroquois, when a man married, he brought his belongings to his wife's lodge and lived with her family. Each Mandan lodge housed twenty to forty people in all.

Dome-shaped, the houses were spacious and comfortable, measuring some forty to eighty feet (12.1 to 24.3m) in circumference. The houses were partially subterranean, with the lower part extending two feet (60.9cm) into the ground. Inside, the excavated earth formed a raised border against the inner walls. The lodge thus remained warm and draft-free in winter and cool in summer. People used the lodge's slightly flattened roof as a cool porch where they could relax and visit on hot summer nights.

They also used their roofs for drying maize and for storing the women's bull boats. These were round, basin-shaped boats made of rawhide stretched over a willow frame. A drag, made of driftwood and attached to the bison tail (which was left on the hide), kept the boat on course. A single paddler could successfully steer the boat.

Various forms of worship permeated the Indians' daily lives; they believed that only by continuously acknowledging the Sacred Powers could they maintain harmony and well-being. They offered up many prayers to the Creator every day. A prayer could be as simple as giving thanks at sunrise or offering a morsel of food to the Earth and Sky before eating, or as complex as performing a lengthy ceremony.

Every summer the Mandan celebrated their major tribal ceremony, the four-day Okipa ceremony. This ceremony, which included a vision quest and a celebration recalling the creation of the Mandan people, ensured prosperity for the coming year by giving thanks to the Sacred Powers. Dressed as mythological figures in the story of Mandan creation, older men recited tribal myths in the Okipa lodge while young men fasted

ing cornstalks circled a cooking fire. The first ears of corn were boiled and placed on a scaffold above the fire as an offering of thankfulness to the Creator. Then the celebrants buried the ashes, built a new fire, and boiled more corn to share among everyone in the village.

A warrior-chief and a civil-chief were in charge of each village. Although they were capable warriors, the Mandan preferred peaceful trading relations with their neighbors. The Hidatsa admired bravery and celebrated a young man's first battle trophy—a stolen horse or a scalp. But if a single warrior was lost without compensating enemy deaths, the Hidatsa did not perform a scalp dance and the war leader remained in mourning until the victim's family forgave him.

Mandan women were admired for their strength as well as their beauty. Women farmed,

# THE VISION QUEST

The vision quest was a profoundly important event in a young Indian's life; indeed, a boy's experience during his vision quest determined his image of himself and his role in life. His vision was intensely personal, a direct encounter with the Great Spirit or Great Mystery Power, who could appear in any form. Spiritual preparation—days of fasting, prayer, and cleansing of mind and body—prepared him for this significant event. Since childhood he had been raised to revere the mystical reality that is always present beneath surface appearances, and taught to see with his heart rather than only with his eyes.

The immense power of the experience is clear from the description of one Sioux boy:

> Blackness...all around me [that] cut me off from the outside world, even from my own body [and] made me listen to the voices from within me... I felt the presence of my forefathers...as I cried out to the Grandfather Spirit until, at last, he granted me my dream.

*A prayer cloth blows in the wind of Bear Butte, South Dakota. These long strips of colored cloth were tied to the base of a tree during a vision quest.*

and prepared themselves spiritually for the ordeal that would produce their life-shaping visions. The young men, skewered through their chests, hung from the roof of the lodge until they fainted. Meanwhile, outside the lodge, Buffalo Society members danced around the village plaza's ceremonial post. They were soon joined by Okipa Society elders, also dressed as mythological figures, who led the vision-seeking young men around the central post, trailing buffalo skulls. Through their self-imposed torture, young men offered the ultimate sacrifice to the Sacred Powers by demonstrating their unquestioning faith in their religion. By completing this feat of endurance, they helped to unite the tribe in worship and to ensure the survival of their people in the year ahead.

Pawnee life was also organized around farming, especially for corn. In addition, they, too, hunted buffalo. They covered their log lodges with earth and grass, a sod construction later imitated by settlers from Europe because such houses were warm in winter's bitter cold and cool in summer's intense heat.

The Osage, Kansa, Omaha, and Missouri originally lived along the northern tributaries of the Mississippi until they were pushed out of the area by eastern tribes fleeing the well-armed Iroquois. Like the Mandan and the Pawnee, they quickly adapted to a Plains life of farming and gathering with some buffalo hunting.

*Plains warriors drive buffalo off a cliff in a "buffalo jump," the popular method of hunting before the arrival of horses. Below: A Plains Indian painting by an unknown artist shows a row of prancing horses whose riders wear buffalo horns.*

# THE HORSE NATIONS

*My horses, prancing they are coming.*
*My horses, neighing they are coming;*
*Prancing, they are coming.*
*All over the universe they come.*
*They will dance; may you behold them.*
*A horse nation, they will dance.*
  **—Black Elk**

The Sioux came to the Plains by a less direct route than that of the other Indian nations: before the fourteenth century they moved into what is now Minnesota, Wisconsin, and Manitoba, Canada, where they multiplied until their increasing population forced many bands farther west in a series of migrations. By the seventeenth and early eighteenth cen-

turies, these peoples were living a semi-settled life, broken by summer and autumn buffalo hunts. The arrival of the horse, brought to the Plains by whites in the eighteenth century, completely transformed the Sioux way of life. Settled village life seemed dull once they discovered that they could mount horses and ride with the wind, darting among buffalo herds and raiding other tribes.

Other Plains dwellers, the Crow, Arapaho, and Cheyenne, also responded to the arrival of the horse by altering their ways of life. The Cheyenne and Crow were once village farmers, while the Shoshone and Comanche had been Great Basin hunter-gatherers. To all the Plains Indians, the horse brought greater mobility. Since movement was simpler to accomplish, it was no longer necessary for the people to live in settled villages; in addition, mobility made it much easier to hunt buffalo.

Until about 1750, moving camp had been a lengthy and exhausting experience with groups moving a distance of only about five to six miles (8 to 9.6km) each day. Each family used a dog to pull a travois that held the family's folded tipi. One dog could carry about 75 pounds (34kg). The dogs, however, were unreliable because they often took off to chase rabbits or to fight each other. The rest of the family's belongings went on another travois or on the shoulders and backs of the women. Those who could not walk—the old and the infirm—usually had to be left behind.

A horse, however, could travel twice as far in a day and carry four times the load of a dog. Old and sick people who were unable to walk could

now be carried on a horse-drawn travois. Tipis became larger because horses could haul longer, heavier lodgepoles. Lodges, originally formed using six to eight bison skins—the limits of a dog's carrying capacity—expanded to twelve or more hides. The horse also made it possible to transport larger amounts of belongings and food, such as dried meat and berries.

The arrival of the horse completely transformed the bison hunt. Before horses were available, hunters working on foot used to stampede bison over a cliff. In early spring through autumn, the hunters would build bison traps, which consisted of two lines of piled stones stretching for two miles (3.2km) in a V-shaped formation, with the narrower end funneling toward the edge of a cliff. The hunters would set a grass fire or use beaters on the herd to work the frightened animals into a stampede; they then drove the animals between the

*A Blackfeet warrior poses in ceremonial dress astride his horse. The acquisition of horses completely altered the lifestyles of many Plains peoples.*

## SOME USES OF THE BISON

1. Tongue: Meat, hairbrushes
2. Skull: Ceremonies, prayer
3. Horns: Cups, spoons, ladles, headdresses
4. Muscles and sinew: Bows, thread
5. Hair: Headdresses, pillows, rope, halters, bridles
6. Bones: Knives, arrowheads, quirts, awls, dice, splints
7. Hide (tanned): Moccasins, bedding (with hair), clothing, bags, tipi linings
8. Hide (raw): Parfleches, headdresses, clothing, glue, rattles
9. Dung: Fuel, signals
10. Tail: Flyswatters, tipi decoration
11. Paunch: Cooking pots, water container
12. Hooves: Rattles, glue

Native women turned almost every portion of the bison into food, clothing, shelter, and many other useful items. Meat was either eaten fresh or dried and pounded with berries into pemmican. Hides became clothing, bedding, tipis, shields, or parfleches that held food, clothing, and other articles. Women used the animal's paunch, or stomach, supported by four poles, as a cooking pot for stew. The tendons that run along the bison's backbone and legs were used as thread for sewing. Hair provided material for horses' bridles. Bowls were carved out of bison horn.

two lines of stones to the cliff. The hunt had to be carried out close to home because of the difficulty in transporting the killed bison on dog travois and on the hunters' backs.

Horses allowed the Indians to kill bison more easily and with less waste because the hunters no longer had to stampede entire herds over cliffs. A single hunter riding a buffalo-runner—a well-trained horse with great endurance—would use a bow and arrow (later, a rifle) to kill three to four bison in one day, providing enough meat to feed his family for several months.

The hunters sought buffalo not only to supply their families with much-needed meat, but also for the thrill of the hunt itself, the excitement of riding in a herd of buffalo in full flight amid the deafening thunder of thousands of buffalo hooves. A Sioux warrior, Standing Bear, recalled the excitement of one of his first hunts:

I was thirteen years old and supposed to be a man, so I made up my mind I'd get a yearling. One of them went down a draw and I raced after him on my pony. My first shot did not seem to hurt him at all; but my pony kept right after him, and the second arrow went in halfway. I think I hit his heart, for he began to wobble as he ran and blood came out of his nose. Hunters cried, "Yuhoo!" once when they killed, but this was my first bison, and I just kept on yelling "Yuhoo!" People must have thought I was killing a whole herd, the way I yelled.

It is easy to understand why the famous Sioux leader Red Cloud (1822–1909) said that the buffalo—the source of food, shelter, tools, and fuel—was a sacred gift from the Creator to the Sioux people. A Sioux named Lame Deer explained how the buffalo came to the people in the story of White Buffalo Woman. As soon as she had vanished over the horizon:

> buffalo in great herds appeared, allowing themselves to be killed so that the people might survive. And from that day on, our relations, the buffalo, furnished the people with everything they needed—meat for their food, skins for their clothes and tipis, bones for their many tools.

To the Sioux in particular, the buffalo is the embodiment of the power of the sun; when the Sioux followed the buffalo, they were following the sun on earth. By following the sun and the buffalo, the Sioux helped to stay in balance and live in harmony with the sacred powers of the universe.

A warrior prized his warhorse because its endurance and fleetness meant the difference between life and death. He painted both himself and his pony for war, adding scalp locks to his horse's bridle, red ribbons to its head, and eagle feathers to its mane or tail. He allowed no one else to ride his warhorse, which he kept tethered beside his tipi.

The horse also transformed the lives of Plains women. A woman's value was measured in the number of horses her potential bridegroom gave her father. Women often owned their own horses: Blackfeet women even bartered for better mounts to improve their extensive herds. Comanche women rode hard, competing with the men in bringing down game on antelope hunts.

Dropping all elements of a settled lifestyle, Plains Indians embraced mobility as a way of life, leaving their villages to range over vast areas. Household objects, which now had to be carried from place to place, were made to be light, durable, and portable. The Plains people lived in portable

*A Plains warrior uses his horse's body to shield himself from enemy fire, hooking his heel over the horse's back and resting his elbow in a rope looped around the horse's neck. The rider could then shoot arrows under the horse's neck or over its back.*

*Once sturdy Indian ponies replaced dogs in travois harnesses, moving camp was much easier. Horses could bear the load of larger tipis and heavier household goods.*

## TRAVOIS

*The travois was also used to provide a ride for the very young, the sick, and the elderly.*

The travois, originally used in a smaller version on dogs, was built by placing two poles on either side of a horse and harnessing the apparatus to the animal's chest, shoulders, and back. Crossbars covered with hides joined the poles behind the animal as the rear end of the poles dragged on the ground.

tipis, and they could pack their belongings in skin containers, load them on horse-drawn travois, and move quickly. The nineteenth-century artist George Catlin described watching a Sioux encampment of six hundred lodges strike camp, pack, and move within minutes:

> In one minute six hundred [lodges] were seen waving and flapping in the wind, and in one minute more all were flat upon the ground.... Each [horse and dog] was speedily loaded... and ready to fall into the grand procession.

In order to maintain this lifestyle, the people of the nomadic Plains tribes devoted themselves to the daily care, protection, and breeding of large herds of horses. It is easy to understand why wealth came to be measured in horses.

While the men supplied their families with meat, the women were responsible for maintaining their households and for moving the camp. Plains men made decisions in the outside world, while women ruled the tipis as well as exercised considerable behind-the-scenes influence in major tribal decisions. The women of the family owned the tipi and household furniture (such as backrests made from peeled willow rods), as well as the kettle, tripod, containers of dried meat, and any fresh meat their husbands secured while out hunting.

To make a tipi measuring 12 to 16 feet (3.6 to 4.8m) in diameter, eight to twelve bison skins were required. The construction of a new tipi was a social event similar to a sewing bee and usually took place in the summer camp when there was an abundance of hides. With enough assistance, a woman could make a tipi in a single day.

An older woman who was an experienced lodge-maker helped the woman who needed the tipi to cut the skins to the correct size and shape. Other women then joined to help them sew the skins together with sinew, all of them talking and singing as they sewed. The sewing began after the hostess had served a meal to her assistants; the completion of the tipi was followed by another meal.

The women placed poles over the tipi's tripod base, leaving the top open for a smoke hole. When the tipi was erected, the sacred hearth fire, a gift from the sun of its life-giving warmth, would rest directly beneath the smoke hole. Smoke flaps for ventilation were attached to long poles over the smoke hole at the top of the tipi and could be closed in rainy weather or adjusted to changes in the wind direction. Often a woman noted for her cheerful disposition worked on the smoke flaps; the influence of her personality was thought to efficiently guide the smoke out of the newly constructed tipi.

Families used stones to hold the bottom edges of the tipi in place, but in the summer they often rolled up the cover to allow a cooling breeze to circulate. They covered the doorway with a flap of skin and hung an inner lining of skin 4 to 5 feet (1.2 to 1.5m) high from the tipi poles to the ground to help insulate the tipi against snow and cold winter winds.

When visiting a family in their tipi, a visitor had to obey strict rules of behavior. An open door meant that you could enter the tipi directly, but a closed door meant that you should announce your presence and wait for the owner to invite you inside. Once a male visitor entered the tipi, he went to the right and waited for the host to invite him to sit in the guest place on the owner's left side at the rear of the tipi. A woman entered after the man and went to the left. Guests were expected to bring their own bowls and spoons and to eat all they were given when they were invited to a feast. The host signaled his guests to leave by cleaning his pipe.

Although the tipi could be chilly during the harsh Plains winters, it was the perfect home for the nomadic Plains Indians. When it was time to move, the women used the tipi's poles as the sidebars of a horse-drawn travois and lashed the tipi cover on a willow framework platform to the travois.

As much as the tipi seems synonymous with the Indians of the Plains, they were not the only people to use it. The Woodland peoples of North America and Asia also used tipis but covered them with sheets of bark or branches or with moose hides. Some of these people used tipis only as temporary hunting shelters.

*A Plains tipi, or "a good mother," so called because she protected her children so well.*

*Arapaho women tan a hide on the Wind River Reservation. After removing the tissue and hair, they scraped and smoothed the hide, later softening it by rubbing it with a mixture of buffalo brains and fat.*

Like most aspects of Indian life, the tipi had spiritual significance. Symbolically, it represented the world: the floor was the Earth, the walls the Sky, and the tipi poles were the trails from the Earth to the Spirit World. Between the rear of the tipi and the central fire was a space considered sacred to Mother Earth. There the family burned incense—sweetgrass, cedar, or sage—so that its fragrant smoke carried the prayers of the people up to the Spirit World.

The Plains people decorated the exterior of the tipis with painted designs that depicted such things as the family totem (an animal or other natural symbol sacred to that family), historic events, personal visions, or spiritual designs such as celestial constellations. A village of decorated tipis was a magnificent sight. Depending upon space, the tipis were arranged in a circle or circles. When the various groups of a tribe joined together for a large encampment, for example, the tipis might have been arranged in a series of concentric circles. The pattern of location was organized according to family groups, and each woman knew exactly where to place her lodge.

In 1970, an old woman on the Rosebud Reservation in South Dakota described the tipis she remembered: "What a wonderful sight it was on a dark night, the many tipis glowing faintly red from the fires within....These tipis were so alive, breathing almost with the blue-white smoke rising from them...."

Everything the Plains Indians owned was lightweight and easily transportable. They made saddlebags as well as other storage containers for personal belongings from light and durable rawhide or tanned skins.

The Cheyenne and Crow once made pottery, but when they became more nomadic, pottery was too fragile, so they replaced it with skin containers and wood and bone utensils. Their furniture, such as the willow backrest, was also lightweight and collapsible. They carried water in buffalo paunches and packed their food in parfleches—stiff, light, rawhide envelopes.

Parfleche designs show how deeply art and spirituality were intertwined in the routine of living. Women painted the parfleche with an hourglass figure (two triangles joined at their apexes) that represented a prayer from Earth (the lower triangle) going to heaven (the upper triangle). Stars—which the Lakota Sioux called "the holy speech of the Great Spirit"—met the prayer where the Earth and Sky join, represented by the intersection of the two triangles.

Women made clothing from deer and elk hides. Sacred beliefs dictated exactly how the hides should be handled while the garments were being made. A woman had to fold hides in a precise way when she was making a dress. In winter, men wore a shirt, breechclout, and high leggings. Women

# ARTS AND CRAFTS

*A Crow skin, decorated with a male and female elk and their tracks.*

Plains tribes were well known for their clothes and horse trappings made of bison skins and decorated with porcupine quill embroidery and, later, with beaded designs. The first beads used were blue, black, and white pony beads, with which women created bold designs in black and white or blue and white. After 1830, seed beads, which were smaller and came in more colors, became popular. By 1870, translucent beads were available. These beads were smaller than pony beads but larger than seed beads and came in even richer colors and a variety of shapes. Beaded garments were quite heavy: a beaded shirt could weigh 4 pounds (1.8kg).

Each Plains tribe used distinct designs and techniques, traditions that continue among today's beadworkers. In the Southern Plains, the Kiowa and Comanche favor light, delicate bead trim. Kiowa designs also have a beaded abstract floral element made using an overlay stitch technique and the gourd or peyote stitch, which is actually a form of bead netting. It is believed that the Kiowa learned both techniques when the Delaware Indians from the East Coast moved to the Texas area

in 1829. In contrast to the Kiowa, the Sioux of North and South Dakota cover large areas of clothing with beads. Sioux, Cheyenne, and Arapaho designs tend to be geometric.

Most groups also painted rawhide articles such as parfleche containers, shields, tipis, tipi linings, and robes.

In addition, the Plains peoples are known for their stone and wood carving, including elaborate stone pipes and beautiful wooden flutes.

Featherwork was another important craft. The Plains Indians were famed for their flowing feather war bonnets. They also used feathers to decorate shields, pipe stems, coup sticks, banners, shirts, and leggings. For particular dances, they made large bustles of feathers, which are often seen today at intertribal powwows.

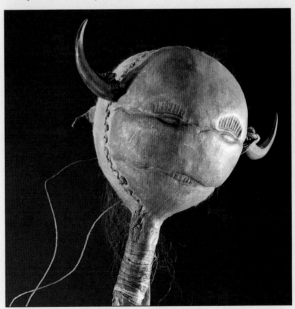

*A rawhide rattle in the shape of a buffalo head features horns made of claws, possibly bear.*

wore a skin dress and shorter leggings. Both wore moccasins and bison-skin robes.

The Plains Indians decorated their clothing, as well as everyday objects, with paint or with sewn porcupine quills. The stems of maidenhair fern, grasses, and later corn husks were sometimes substituted for porcupine quills. After the Indians acquired glass trade beads from the Europeans in the early 1800s, beading began to replace quillwork.

The beads were available in bright colors and were easier to apply than bird or porcupine quills, which had to be dyed and flattened before they could be sewn onto hide clothing. Before contact with the whites, Indians had access to natural dyes in shades of brown, red, yellow, and some blue and green. Later, commercial pigments were introduced.

Art was an integral part of daily life for all Indians. Both men and women painted, with men

*Sissiton Sioux Wa-kan-wa-ya-ka-pi wears a headdress made of carefully pre-pared eagle feathers laced to a tradecloth headband. Such elabo-rate headdresses gave a dramatic, sometimes fearsome, appearance to a rider on horseback.*

specializing in painting war exploits in a picto-graphic style on bison robes, tipis, and tipi liners. Women painted bison hides in more geometric designs and created the quill- and beadwork. After Indians moved to reservations, they began drawing in ledgers and notebooks for their own use. They also began painting small deer hides, elk skins, and miniature tipi covers for sale.

After they acquired the horse, the Plains Indians also changed their clothing so that it became the most elaborate, highly decorated dress of any Native Americans. Women began to make richly decorated saddles and harnesses as well as more elaborate dress clothing to enhance their appearance on horse-back. Fringe looked beautiful moving through the wind and helped to shed water off the buckskin.

Having mastered the horse and made hunting more efficient, Plains men had more time available, which they used to participate in ceremonial activi-ties, to raid enemy camps for horses, and to prac-tice their skills as warriors. Engaging in war between tribes had long been a common activity among the Plains people and was an important means of gaining prestige. The long history of war-fare on the Plains had given rise to many customs and rituals: the correct practice of war allowed the warriors to earn honors. With the arrival of the horse, warfare also changed, and its practices became far more elaborate, partially because riding on horseback made closer combat possible. This meant that there were greater opportunities for the warriors to earn war honors. In the past, the actions of the warring group as a whole had determined the prestige of the warriors; now individual feats of bravery became as important as, if not more impor-tant than, the final result of a battle. The amount of courage it took to perform a particular deed in war-fare determined the degree of honor awarded.

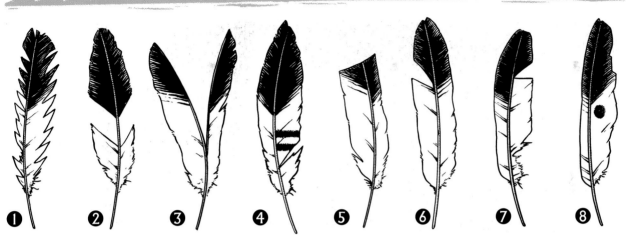

❶   ❷   ❸   ❹   ❺   ❻   ❼   ❽

*Friend or foe could learn a warrior's war deeds and honors with a glance at the feathers the warrior wore in his hair. Notched or serrated feathers (1, 2, 4) announced how many times he had counted coup; a split feather (3) meant that he had been wounded many times; a feather clipped on the diagonal (5) or notched (6, 7) meant that he had cut his foe's throat or taken his scalp; a red spot (8) meant that he had killed an enemy.*

The act of "counting coup" (from the French word for "blow")—which involved touching an enemy or capturing a personal possession such as his war shirt—was among the most valued of war honors. A coup stick was a long slender branch that a warrior used to touch an enemy. There was a much greater risk and therefore a greater display of courage involved in touching the enemy with a coup stick than in shooting him long distance with an arrow or bullet. Indians later had difficulty in adjusting to the white manner of warfare, which valued the final outcome over individual acts of courage or honor. Because of the dangerous nature of war, it was a deeply spiritual event, full of ritual: men rode to war protected by medicine bundles and medicine shields, and covered their horses with sacred gopher dust. They painted themselves with lightning designs that were intended to make the wearer bulletproof and to give his horse supernatural speed.

While their parents were busy hunting, raiding, or taking care of the household, children had great freedom, including the freedom to learn from their

## PLAINS INDIAN SHIELDS

A Plains Indian shield reflects both nomadic Plains culture and the qualities of the individual who made it. Those who carried shields were warriors whose lives revolved around feats of bravery and extraordinary courage. The shield embodied the protective power given the warrior by Wakan Tanka, power that would see him through battles of defeat and glory.

Kiowa author N. Scott Momaday explained, "In a real sense the Plains warrior is his shield. It is his personal flag...the object of his holiest quest, the tangible expression of his deepest being."

Plains shields had a diameter of about 24 inches (60.9cm) and were usually made of bison hides, so thick and tough that they could repel stones, arrows, bullets, and clubs. Although the shield provided a degree of physical protection, its

*A warrior's shield design often came to him during a vision quest. The buffalo tracks on the shield embody the powers of fleetness and endurance.*

true protective power was spiritual, for the shield was powerful medicine as it announced to the enemy: you have now entered the presence of my power.

*A Lakota Indian stands outside a modern sweat lodge at the Rosebud Reservation.*

mother had the village crier invite everyone to a feast or gave away a horse in the girl's honor. In most tribes, girls were isolated from the rest of the village at this time because they were believed to be in contact with a powerful spirit. The girl's mother or another older woman taught the young woman how to make moccasins and to perform other traditional female tasks. The privileges and duties of womanhood now belonged to her.

A Plains Indian boy also experienced isolation during his initiation into adulthood. He went alone on a vision quest, seeking direct contact with the Great Spirit, which could appear in many forms. Through this experience, he received spiritual guidance and helpers who would be with him throughout his life. He undertook his first vision quest at puberty but repeated it whenever he needed help from the Great Spirit. Women could go on vision quests as well.

The vision-seeker first purified himself in a sweat lodge, a low dome made of willow saplings covered with buffalo skins (today, blankets, canvas, or plastic are also used). Inside the sweat lodge was a pile of red-hot rocks, over which the vision-seekers poured cold water to create steam. A medicine person sang prayer chants to help the Indians focus on releasing old thoughts, memories, or experiences that might keep them from being in touch with the spiritual aspects of life. In this way, sweat baths cleared the mind and body, leaving a person pure and ready for contact with the Great Spirit.

The Indians of nearly every region used tobacco pipes, but for the Plains Indians, such pipes were among the most important of sacred objects. Individuals owned their own pipes, and the tribes also kept very elaborate pipes that were used only for special ceremonies, which were performed for reasons such as ensuring a successful bison hunt, healing, or marking the beginning of peace or war. Pipes were usually made of a highly valued stone known as red pipestone (catlinite). The Indians also made pipes of other materials, including shale, soapstone, calcite, chlorite, steatite, argillite, lime-

experiences. They were not pampered or overly protected; neither were they harshly disciplined. Aunts, uncles, and grandparents helped with parenting so that children were surrounded by a network of affectionate relatives but were not overly attached to one person. For the children, daily activities included games as well as work. Children learned about their adult roles through sports and games. Boys learned to hunt with small bows and arrows and developed speed by running footraces. Girls played with dolls and toy tipis.

As with all Native American groups, the peoples of the Great Plains experienced the spiritual world as a part of everyday life, believing that the Great Spirit created life and existed as part of every living thing: stones, earth, trees, birds, sky, and human beings. Ceremonial rituals provided a way to honor the Great Spirit and to seek personal contact and guidance from this power.

Among the Plains peoples, puberty was a time for great spiritual and social celebration. When a Sioux or Cheyenne girl reached puberty, her

## PASTIMES AND GAMES

Plains boys hunted small game with miniature bows. As soon as their skills improved, they joined their elders in the buffalo hunt. Running games encouraged agility and speed. Crow chief Plenty Coups described an experience from his childhood when his grandfather ordered him to catch a butterfly: "In and out among the trees and bushes, across streams...the dodging butterfly led me far before I caught it." His grandfather then told him to reverently "rub its wings over your heart, my son, and ask the butterflies to lend you their grace and swiftness."

Girls played with dolls and toy tipis, and they often participated, as well, in the rougher games that boys played.

In the winter, fathers made sleds out of buffalo ribs for their children. Polished by sliding over the snow, the bones became smoother than the steel runners of modern sleds.

Older people enjoyed sleight-of-hand games with a marked and an unmarked object that one player concealed in his hands as his opponents tried to guess which hand held the unmarked object. Sometimes this game lasted all night. The player who held the markers did his best to confuse his opponents, while songs and dances accompanied the action in order to addle the side that was guessing which hand held the unmarked object.

Women especially enjoyed dice games. The Sioux carved and painted lizards, spiders, and turtles on dice made of bone. The different designs had different values, and points were rewarded for the design that landed upward when a woman tossed the dice into the air from a round basket. Women wagered their beaded chokers and hair ties on the result.

stone, and serpentine slate for the pipe bowl, with ash or sumac for the stem. Some special pipes were carved into ornate sculptured shapes.

The Sioux Lame Deer described his feelings when he was allowed to smoke his tribe's Buffalo Calf pipe:

> I felt the pipe coming alive in my hand...a power surging from it into my body, filling all of me....When I smoked it I was at the center of all things, giving myself to the Great Spirit....Every other Indian praying with this pipe would...feel the same.

When the chokecherries ripened in the summer, the Lakota Sioux and other Plains peoples held a ceremony to thank the Great Spirit for all the blessings of the previous year and to pray for prosperity, health, and happiness in the year to come. The Sun Dance, a ceremony of spiritual renewal and rededication, lasted nearly two weeks and included specific rituals and dances, such as the Buffalo Dance, which celebrated the blessings of home and human fertility.

For the first four days, the Sun Dance was a festive social occasion: the various bands of the tribe

*Left: The pipestone (catlinite) quarry on the Coteau des Prairies, 1836–1837. Above: An ornately carved catlinite Sioux pipe.*

## PROPHECY

Long before the whites invaded Lakota country, a holy man named Wooden Cup prophesied their coming as well as the disappearance of the buffalo. He also claimed that whites would "entangle this world with iron"—railroads—and that little square gray houses would be imposed on the land. His prophecies taught that such events were inevitable, making the outward defeat of Lakota culture part of a cosmic plan and lifting the burden of responsibility from Indians and whites alike.

came from all over the Plains to be together during this summer encampment. After being separated during the long winter, friends and relatives were excited to see one another and to tell stories about all that had happened during the past year. Young people began courtships, parents arranged marriages, and people exchanged property to renew ties of kinship.

During the second four-day period, the people were involved in preparations for the most sacred time, the final four days. A group of men who had volunteered to dance would stay away from the others during this preparatory period, receiving instructions from the shamans on the rituals to come. The final section of the festival began with the "capture" of a cottonwood tree, which would be the ceremonial centerpiece. On the second sacred day, a group of virtuous women went on a ritual search for the captured tree. At first, the women would pretend that they could not locate the tree; then they would find it on their fourth try. A ceremonial procession brought back the tree.

On the third day the people prepared for the next day's ceremonies by painting and decorating the tree with sacred objects. Men joined in a war dance around the tree.

On the final day, shamans greeted the sun at dawn and then assisted the dancers in their final preparations, painting them with symbols related to the severity of the ordeal they had chosen to endure. Some dancers simply fasted and danced around the pole as long as they could. Others sacrificed pieces of their flesh. The most respected men were those who had skewers inserted through their flesh. Some dragged buffalo skulls attached to the skewers while others were suspended from the fork of the central Sun Dance pole. Suffering through the extraordinary pain helped each participant to experience personal contact with the Great Spirit, bringing prestige to himself and well-being to his entire tribe.

*Short Bull's painting of the Sun Dance features four teams of dancers surrounding a large open circle. The circle's center is marked by the sacred Sun Dance Tree.*

*Quanah Parker (1845–1911) greets rancher Charles Goodnight in front of the Comanche encampment. Parker became the first recognized chief of all Comanche in 1875, and later visited Washington, D.C., as a delegate for his people.*

## EUROPEAN CONTACT

*I could see that the [whites] did not care for each other the way our people did....They would take everything from each other if they could, and so there were some who had more of everything than they could use, while crowds of people had nothing at all and maybe were starving. They had forgotten that the earth was their mother.*

**—Black Elk**

The white man had brought the horse that made possible the nomadic lifestyle of the Plains peoples; the white man also brought to an end this glorious period, which lasted only slightly longer than a century. The problems began in the mid-eighteenth century, when English and French trappers reached the eastern Plains.

Encouraged by reports of abundant game in the west, hundreds of trappers in search of beaver pelts began to flood the Plains. These mountain men generally shared the Indians' love of space and freedom, and their activities did not endanger the Indians' way of life. The traders who followed them, however, saw the Indians as merely a large, untapped source of profit. The traders brought whiskey, knives, guns, blankets, and kettles. Over time, as many Indians became dependent on these items, their self-sufficient way of life was undermined. The traders also provided firearms to some tribes, thereby giving those tribes a much greater advantage in warfare, which upset the balance of power among various Plains peoples.

Whites brought sicknesses, too, such as measles, diphtheria, and smallpox. Groups such as the Mandan, who had become shrewd traders and had the closest contact with the whites, were ravaged most by such diseases. By 1837, the Mandan tribe, once 3,600 strong, was reduced to 125 people.

## THE INTER TRIBAL BISON COOPERATIVE

*In the Sioux tradition, the buffalo is the keeper of women, symbolic of generosity and kindness.*

The Sioux people say that when the First Buffalo came out of a cave far to the north, he was wearing a white robe. According to author Jacqueline Sletto, the Buffalo told the Indians, "My tribe and I will come back to you in great multitudes. Use us well, for one day, we will go back to the mountains again. And when we have gone, the Indians will be no more."

Today, the 27 tribes of the Inter Tribal Bison Cooperative are working to bring the bison back to Indian tribal lands. Cheyenne, Sioux, Crow, Shoshone, and Navajo are purchasing buffalo and learning buffalo management.

By reintroducing the bison, the ITBC hopes to reestablish the ecological balance of the Plains, which has been upset by overgrazing and range depletion from cattle ranching. Unlike cattle, buffalo crop the grass but leave untouched the tall coarse growth that shelters birds, mice, and other small animals. In addition, buffalo droppings fertilize the soil, while cattle dung acidifies it; buffalo hooves aerate the soil, while cattle hooves pack it down. Their shaggy winter coats are ideal protection for germinating seeds: when the buffalo shed each spring, the seeds fall to earth in tufts of buffalo hair.

In addition to revitalizing the prairie ecosystem, reintroducing the buffalo may increase Indian income as buffalo meat (leaner and higher in protein than beef) becomes more popular. Artisans will also have buffalo robes, rattles, and skulls. Most importantly, this is an opportunity for the Plains tribes to reestablish their spiritual relationship with the buffalo.

By 1850, a steady stream of white settlers was passing through the Plains on their way to California and Oregon. The vast influx of whites began with gold-seeking forty-niners and farmers. Many settlers decided to stay on the Great Plains. Few of them had respect for tribal customs. Forts were built to protect the whites, and the government forced Indians to sign peace treaties they did not understand.

In 1851, near Fort Laramie, Wyoming, the United States government called a meeting of some 10,000 Indians in an effort to secure guarantees of safety for the whites using the Oregon Trail and to end the inter-tribal warfare that had claimed the lives and livestock of white settlers. The Superintendent of Indian Affairs established tribal territories within which each nation could hunt exclusively. Tribal leaders agreed to this arrangement although the concept was alien to their entire way of life, and it soon became clear that they had not understood the terms. In exchange for the safe passage of settlers along the Oregon Trail and the permission to build forts, the government agreed to distribute payment in the form of trade goods such as blankets and provisions.

The whites asked the Sioux to name a single leader who was to be responsible for all of them. The Sioux, with their three main groups divided into many bands, had no single head chief. Tribes were simply not organized in the same way as white governments—leadership was earned through a different process. Under pressure from the whites, the Sioux nevertheless chose Conquering Bear, a trade chief, to be their "leader," but this action was essentially meaningless because the real leaders continued to be the individual chiefs of each group.

In 1854, peace was shattered when a starving cow belonging to Mormon emigrants wandered into a Sioux camp. Its owner told the soldiers at Fort Laramie that the Indians had stolen it. Although the Sioux offered payment for the animal, the emigrants refused, demanding punishment of the offending

## TANTOO CARDINAL

Tantoo Cardinal is a part Cree, part Chippewa actress. Her grandfather was a member of Big Bear's tribe, one of the last in northern Canada to sign a treaty with the government. She explained the differences between white and Indian views of the world:

Our way of understanding life, our concept of the earth as a living being, was alien to the people who came here. They knew so much, they didn't have anything to learn from us. And that gave them permission to see us as ignorant.

People came to North America for religious freedom, and where did the land come from to live on? From people who are persecuted. Our children were taken away and put in boarding schools so they wouldn't grow up to be Indian. Our language was outlawed; we were not allowed to pray in the Indian way, or wear Indian clothing, or live in the Indian way. That was a conscious thing: we have to make these people into white people.

Maybe in their own way they were saying, our way of life is good and you should have that. But it was not love that did those things. When your spiritual freedom is taken away, that's the water of your soul.

*Tantoo Cardinal (far right), playing a Huron woman in the movie* **Black Robe.**

Indians. Hungry for glory, the commanding officer, Lieutenant Grattan, insisted on marching into the Indian village with a detachment of soldiers. Despite repeated warnings that he was creating a serious incident out of a trivial matter, Grattan lined up his men on either side of their howitzer cannon. He demanded the surrender of the Indian who had killed the old cow. When Conquering Bear refused, soldiers opened fire on the Lakota village, killing a chief. The Sioux swarmed out of their tipis, killing the soldiers. This incident sparked almost three decades of Plains bloodshed.

In 1861, the Civil War drained the forts of experienced soldiers. The government replaced the regular army troops with untrained volunteers. These inexperienced soldiers were no match for the native warriors of the Plains, who took advantage of the military withdrawal. During the final months of the war, conditions became so desperate for the settlers that the Union Army had to use paroled Confederate prisoners to man some of the forts west of the Mississippi. Despite the Indians' best efforts, however, the whites, with their superior weapons and manpower, eventually overcame Indian resistance.

An even more powerful weapon against the Indians of the Great Plains was the ruthless slaughter of the bison. Native lives revolved around this animal, which provided sustenance, clothing, shelter, and all the necessities of everyday life. In 1800, there were some 60 million bison; by 1870 there were only 13 million bison; by 1900 this number had dropped to less than one thousand. In the 1860s, when the railroads were being built, railroad managers hired professional bison hunters to kill enough animals to provide food for the work crews. After the railroads were established, sportsmen regularly shot bison from the railroad coaches as they headed west.

In the 1870s, an East Coast firm started to commercially tan bison hides and sell them as leather. The increased demand for hides sparked a bison-hunting boom. Some professional hunters shot as many as 1,500 bison a week, skinned them, and left the meat to decay in the sun. Sophisticated white tastes also contributed to the slaughter of the buf-

*Left: Sioux survivors of the Battle of the Little Bighorn. Below: A graveyard for United States soldiers who fell in battle sits above a valley in Little Bighorn Park.*

falo: there developed a fashionable rage for smoked bison tongue, and hundreds of thousands of animals were killed for their tongues alone.

Once the bison began to disappear from the Plains, the days of the Indian nations were numbered. Shocked and saddened by the brutal slaughter, the Plains peoples could not understand the senseless waste of the life-giving bison. Sitting Bull explained that the Indians...

> ...kill buffalo as we kill other animals, for food and clothing, and to make our lodges warm....[The whites] kill buffaloes-for what? Go through your country. See the thousands of carcasses rotting on the Plains. Your young

men shoot for pleasure. All they take from a dead buffalo is his tail, or his head, or his horns, perhaps to show they have killed a buffalo. What is this?

The year 1876 marked the greatest and last Indian victory in the ongoing battle with the whites: the famous Battle of the Little Bighorn, also known as Custer's Last Stand. In 1874, Lieutenant Colonel George Armstrong Custer commanded an illegal expedition into the Black Hills—an area known to be profoundly sacred to the Lakota. Treaties signed in 1851 and 1868 had guaranteed that these lands would remain Lakota property, but when Custer claimed—falsely—that there was "gold around the roots of the grass," the area flooded with white prospectors. The government at first tried to buy the land and finally simply took it, leaving the Lakota a dramatically shrunken reservation, devoid of its spiritual center. Disillusioned and despairing, many of the Lakota left the reservation; in response, the government sent the United States Army to find and return the Indians.

Several forces, including one led by Custer, were sent to the Bighorn Valley to remove the Indians. Unknown to them, a very large Indian force was building rapidly in the same location. Indeed, for the first time, the Lakota nation was almost united, as between 1,200 and 3,000 Lakota and Cheyenne warriors camped together on the banks of the Little Bighorn River of eastern Montana. Custer's orders were to determine the size and location of the Indian encampment and to await reinforcements before attacking. Custer had no idea how many warriors were assembled against his approximately six hundred soldiers, yet, foolishly confident of his success, he decided not to wait. Even though the Indian force was probably strong enough to defeat his entire regiment, Custer divided his command: he ordered Captain Frederick W. Benteen to lead 120 troopers to scout far afield; he commanded Major Marcus A. Reno to take 120 men to begin a diversionary attack on the Indian encampment from the south; and he assigned 129 men to guard the pack train.

The legendary Sitting Bull of the Hunkpapa Lakota was responsible for assembling the great concentration of warriors. He was perceptive enough to have recognized the dire straits of the Plains peoples and had decided to try a final, courageous battle. He had summoned the various tribes and they had come, attracted by his great charisma. Many of those who joined were followers of Crazy Horse, one of the most distinguished Oglala war chiefs.

Realizing that they were desperately battling for their entire way of life, the Indians no longer fought primarily for honor and individual glory. Upon encountering Custer and his men, who were

## SITTING BULL

Sitting Bull (1834–1890), one of the best-known Indian leaders, counted his first coup at age fourteen. He grew up to become a respected warrior and medicine man. He led the Sioux to victory at Little Bighorn, an outcome presaged during a vision experienced by Sitting Bull during a Sun Dance, in which he saw white men falling into camp. After Custer's defeat, Sitting Bull led nearly two thousand Sioux to Canada. They later returned to the United States, where his starving people were forced to surrender in 1881, and Sitting Bull was confined to the Standing Rock Reservation in North Dakota. In 1890, white officials, misunderstanding the Ghost Dance, tried to arrest him, and both Sitting Bull and his son, Crow Foot, were shot to death.

strung out in the open, they inflicted as many casualties as possible. Wave after wave of horsemen, led by Gall of the Hunkpapa and Crazy Horse, killed Custer and his troopers long before dusk.

Their victory proved momentary, however, as the government merely hardened its resolve to remove the Indians from the Plains. Over the ensuing months and years, the Indians of the Great Plains were hunted down and killed or forced onto ever-smaller reservations. In 1881, Sitting Bull's band surrendered.

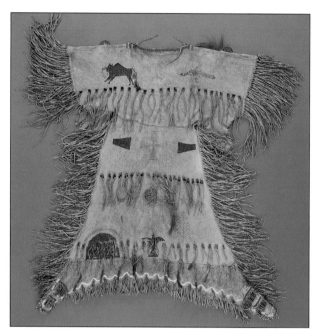

*A girl's Ghost Dance dress. Indians preferred to make Ghost Dance clothing of painted buckskin, similar to what they had worn before white contact.*

Life on the reservations was in some ways even worse than continual flight from the soldiers. The parched land on which the Indians were forced to live was virtually impossible to farm and the rations provided by the government continued to decline, leading to sickness and starvation.

In desperation, many Indians turned to a new movement called the Ghost Dance. In 1889, Wovoka, a Paiute Indian from Nevada, experienced a vision that a new age was coming for the Indians. Participants saw this new world when they sang and danced a circular, shuffling dance that increased in speed until the dancers fell into a trance. Dick Fool Bull explained that the dancers experienced a symbolic death...

...and found themselves walking in a new, beautiful land. They spoke with their parents and grandparents, and with friends that the white soldiers had killed. Their friends were well, and this new world was like the old one, the one the white man had destroyed. It was full of game, full of antelope and buffalo. The grass was green and high, and though long-dead people from other tribes also lived in this new land, there was peace. All the Indian nations formed one tribe and could understand each other.

This new religion, which revitalized Indian hopes, spread across the Great Plains. Many Sioux were convinced that Ghost Dancing would lead to the disappearance of the whites and the return of the bison. They wore special clothing that was supposed to have supernatural power and to be bulletproof. Ideally, such garments were similar to those they had worn before white contact and were made of buckskin painted with visionary Ghost Dance designs. However, they often had to use cloth in place of buckskin, which was becoming more difficult to obtain.

The Ghost Dance was a movement of universal peace; believers felt that the whites would disappear from the land without violence, leaving the world to the Indians. However, white officials and settlers feared the Ghost Dancers, imagining another Indian uprising. In December 1890, troops attempted to arrest Sitting Bull in his cabin, assuming (wrongly) that he was head of the Ghost Dance movement. Sitting Bull and fourteen others were killed in the ensuing scuffle.

## FLOYD RED CROW WESTERMAN

Actor, activist, and singer Floyd Red Crow Westerman was born on a Dakota Sioux reservation and remembers tribal celebrations:

*I'd spend all my energy running around with all of the other kids where everyone was dancing, and then go to sleep in the tent to the sound of the drum beating all night long. Anytime you woke up in the night, you would hear the drum and go back to sleep. So that's still a beautiful sound for me, and it's always a good feeling to go back to those celebrations.*

The last glimmer of hope offered by the Ghost Dance was extinguished when an even greater tragedy occurred later that same month. White authorities had grown increasingly nervous at the frenzied spread of the Ghost Dance and the warlike look of the protective shirts. When the Minneconjou Sioux, led by Big Foot, journeyed to collect rations, the authorities intercepted the travelers and took them to Wounded Knee Creek. There the people began a Ghost Dance. When one Indian fired a concealed gun, panicked soldiers opened fire, killing as many as three hundred men, women, and children. The Wounded Knee massacre broke their spirit: by 1891, armed Sioux resistance had ended.

## LIFE TODAY: PAN-INDIANISM

The mounted Plains warrior, making a stand for the survival of his people and his sacred land, has become a powerful symbol of Indianness. For the Indian, this image has become a symbol of Pan-Indian identity, providing a sense of belonging to a larger group than the individual tribe.

When whites first arrived on this continent, Indians lived in small tribal groups, each of which thought of everyone outside their group as a different order of beings. Other Indians were also outsiders. They had no sense of being an "Indian." The names that groups have for themselves in their own languages reflect this. The Cherokees call themselves a phrase that translates as "Real Human Beings" while the Iroquois refer to themselves as "Men of Men."

With the influx of white settlers, Native American political alliances began to form in various regions by the late 1700s. But it was on the Great Plains that the modern Pan-Indian movement began. The horse made inter-tribal contact possible. Sign language developed to make communication possible among the many Indian peoples who spoke widely different languages.

Beginning with the reservation period of the late 1800s, Plains Indians have had intensive contact with whites. Whites constantly pressured them to assimilate — to accept white customs. In response to this pressure, Pan-Indian movements such as the Ghost Dance spread across the Plains from tribe to tribe. Later, the Native American Church, also known as the Peyote religion, followed a similar path.

To promote assimilation, many young Indians were sent far from home to attend boarding schools with Indians of many different tribes. Most boarding-school Indians came from the Great Plains. Contact with tribal peoples from so many groups made them aware of their identity as Indians as they joined together, finding comfort in each other and their shared identity.

Although they are no longer nomadic, the tribes of the Great Plains continue to be very mobile. The pickup truck has replaced the horse, and Plains Indians will travel hundreds of miles to attend gatherings on other reservations. This kind of mobility furthered their self-awareness and has also encouraged the spread of the Pan-Indian movement.

The universal appeal of Plains culture helps to explain the popularity of such films as *Dances with Wolves*. This movie was unusual in several ways. While other movies have presented a sympathetic portrayal of Indians and have used Native American languages, none has received the wide distribution and public acclaim of this film. Much of the dialogue was in the Lakota (Sioux) language with English subtitles, and the star of the movie, who was white, was required to speak many of his lines in Lakota. This movie also broke new ground in its use of many Native American actors. Finally, this movie was important in its characterization of fully rounded individuals instead of racial stereotypes. Indians were portrayed as intelligent, compassionate, tender people with a wonderful sense of humor.

*Girls gather at a Pan-Indian powwow held on the Fort Berthold Indian Reservation, home to Arikara, Hidatsa, and Mandan tribes.*

# CHAPTER FOUR

# ›THE‹ GREAT BASIN AND THE PLATEAU

*I am tired of fighting. Our chiefs are killed. Looking Glass is dead. It is cold and we have no blankets. The little children are freezing to death. My people, some of them, have run away to the hills and have no blankets, no food; no one knows where they are—perhaps freezing to death. I want to have time to look for my children and see how many I can find. Maybe I shall find them among the dead. Hear me my chiefs. I am tired; my heart is sick and sad. From where the sun now stands, I will fight no more forever.*

—**Surrender speech of Nez Percé Chief Joseph, 1877**

# LANGUAGES OF THE TRIBES OF THE GREAT BASIN AND THE PLATEAU

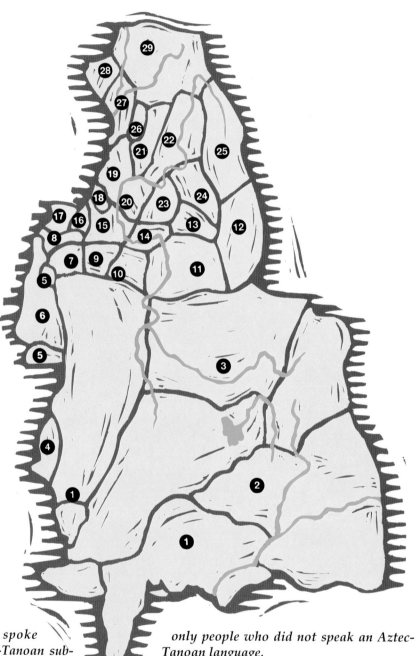

**Great Basin**
1. Paiute
2. Ute
3. Shoshoni
4. Washo

**Plateau**
5. Molala
6. Kalapuya
7. Tenino
8. Chinook
9. Umatilla
10. Cayuse
11. Nez Percé
12. Flathead
13. Coeur
    D'Alene

14. Palouse
15. Yakima
16. Klikitat
17. Cowlitz
18. Kittitas
19. Wenatchi
20. Columbia
21. Okanagan
22. Nespelem
    and Sanpoil
23. Spokane
24. Kalispel
25. Kutenai
26. Nicola
27. Thompson
28. Lillooet
29. Shuswap

*Most of the Great Basin peoples spoke Shoshonean languages in the Aztec-Tanoan subfamily of languages, a major subfamily that includes the Utes of Utah and Colorado and the Aztecs of Mexico. In addition to the Shoshone and the Utes, the Northern Paiute and the Chemehuevi (Southern Paiute) also speak Shoshonean languages. However, these languages were not so similar that the different groups could understand each other. The Washoes who lived near Lake Tahoe were the only people who did not speak an Aztec-Tanoan language.*

*The peoples of the Plateau region spoke languages from four major language families. Groups such as the Nicola spoke Athabascan while the Klikitat, Nez Percé, Umatilla, Yakima, Walla Walla, and Palouse spoke Shahaptin. The Kalispel and the Flathead spoke a Salish language, and groups such as the Kutenai spoke Algonquian.*

The peoples of the Great Basin and the Plateau lived in an area of many contrasts, from the barren, arid reaches of the Great Basin to the bountiful salmon-rich rivers of the Plateau. The generally peaceful peoples of both regions moved with the changing seasons, living primarily by gathering. The more warlike tribes of the Great Plains and the rank-conscious groups of the Northwest Coast bordered the Plateau and Basin regions, influencing the tribes that lived in closest contact with them.

The Great Basin, one of the driest and most inhospitable regions in North America, is a land of desert and salt flats broken by mountains. This area encompasses the land between the Sierra Nevada Mountains in eastern California and the Rocky Mountains in western Colorado, and includes all of Nevada and Utah and parts of California, Oregon, Idaho, Wyoming, Colorado, New Mexico, and Arizona. Wandering tribes lived on the edge of survival by hunting and gathering in this harsh country. They subsisted primarily on a diet of wild seeds and roots, which they supplemented with hunting and fishing.

North of the Great Basin lies the Plateau area, named for the plateaus drained by the Columbia and Fraser river systems. This river system had abundant natural resources, especially salmon and other kinds of fish. The Plateau region stretches into British Columbia, Canada; in the United States, this region includes parts of Oregon, Washington, Idaho, and Montana. In the central part of the Plateau, Native Americans lived in a democratic society free from emphasis on rank. Although they had much in common with the Plains peoples, they were not as driven by inter-tribal warfare.

*Top: Plateau hunters prepare to spear a moose from their canoe. Left: A Flathead mother in Glacier National Park gives her daughter a store-bought doll. The child's playhouse, a miniature buckskin tipi, is behind them.*

# THE MIGRATORY PEOPLES OF THE GREAT BASIN

The peoples of the Great Basin lived in a land where the sun was a blinding, searing power that cracked the Earth, sucking every ounce of moisture from plants, animals, and soil. Mirages shimmered on the horizon as the sand and rock reflected the ovenlike heat of the sun. Every spindly plant, jackrabbit, lizard, and person had to learn to survive with a minimum of water. As they ranged across vast expanses of parched earth in a constant search for food, the peoples of this region always carried a supply of precious water in a pine-gum-coated basket.

The Sierra Nevada Mountains—among America's highest and most rugged ranges—blocked most of the eastbound rain clouds, creating an enormous desert. For many years, these mountains also kept out the westward-bound white settlers, although some exploratory expeditions made it through. In the 1850s, the white prospectors and settlers who journeyed to the area were appalled to see Indians who wore hardly any clothes, ate cater-

pillars and desert rats, and lived only in temporary brush shelters. But these newcomers did not understand how marvelously adapted these hardy survivors were to their rugged terrain.

The native peoples of this region had survived and even thrived in this inhospitable environment for more than 10,000 years. Although they spent their lives in a never-ending search for food and water, their marvelously close observation and understanding of their environment as it changed from month to month kept them alive. They knew precisely where to find the limited sources of food—edible plants and animals—that meant the difference between life and death. In addition to the more than one hundred wild species of seeds, grasses, roots, and similar plants, they also knew some three hundred natural remedies for illness.

The desert's rhythms and the search for food governed every aspect of their lives. Each plant, root, and fish had its place, its proper season when it was

*The rough brush shelters of the nomadic Paiutes. Because they were constantly on the move searching for food, the Paiutes built only rudimentary shelters. The dwellings could even be kept open to the sky because rain seldom fell in the Great Basin.*

ripe or most plentiful. The people followed their food sources each month, with each family using its intimate knowledge of the local area to identify the seasonal growth patterns of all edible plants.

The lack of rainfall not only made growing crops impossible, but also made large game nonexistent. The Great Basin peoples seldom saw the antelope or deer that were plentiful on the Great Plains. Instead, they relied on a wide variety of plants that ripened at different times of year, and the occasional jackrabbit.

The rugged environment supported only small groups, usually a few related families; a harvest of roots, seeds, or buckberries was seldom enough for many people. Only when nature generously provided piñon nuts or rabbits could the Indian groups come together in large communal bands. At such times, they were always careful to store away food for the winter, respecting nature's cycles.

The most joyous time of the year for groups such as the Northern Paiute was autumn, a time when they joined friends they had not seen in many months to harvest the nut of the piñon pine. Scouts would have been searching for many days to locate a grove with enough piñon nuts to feed the groups of families.

The people spent their first sunrise in the piñon forest praying, giving thanks for the coming harvest. They danced in the glow of the campfire the first night to dedicate the first day's harvest. Thanking the Earth for its bounty, they scattered nuts on the ground. Then dancers sang songs of thanksgiving and prayed for enough rain to keep the nuts from drying.

At first light, everyone swarmed through the forest. Men slapped the boughs with long willow poles to shake the cones free. Small boys climbed the trees to knock the cones free with their hands. Young women collected the cones, carrying them back to camp, where the older women pried the nuts free. They roasted the nuts and ground them into a paste to make a creamy, delicious soup.

Men hunted rabbits, the most reliable animal food source, individually throughout the year, but

"...The pinenuts belong to the mountain so we ask the mountain for some of its pinenuts to take home and eat" (traditional Paiute pinenut prayer).

if rabbits were especially plentiful in a given year, the men would conduct a communal rabbit drive in late autumn.

As the drive began, some of the men spread out across the desert to look for rabbits. Others stretched prized rabbit nets—family heirlooms passed from generation to generation—made of milkweed fibers between bushes under the direction of the rabbit-drive boss or chief. Sometimes they set these nets in narrow canyons; at other times, they arranged them in a wide semicircle in the desert. These nets measured 1 to 2 feet (30.4 to 60.9cm) high; some were even a mile (1.6km) in length. When the rabbit boss gave the signal, everyone ran, yelling to scare the jackrabbits into the open. The men tried to channel the rabbits into the netted area so that they could not escape. Men stood at the nets, ready to club the animals as they ran into the fibers of the net or leaped across the enclosed area, trying to escape. Rabbits that did manage to get out of the net were usually caught in the next net: sometimes the Indians used as many as ten to twelve nets. Soon hundreds of rabbits were dead.

As with other game, the people found practical use for nearly every part of the rabbit. They dried some of the meat in the sun and then stored it in

*Tribal members from Utah and Nevada gather to dance at an annual powwow. Such gatherings are important communal and spiritual experiences.*

grass-lined storage pits covered with grass and stones to keep coyotes away. They skinned and boiled the rest of the catch for soup, even pulverizing the bones.

Rabbit skin blankets were especially prized as both clothing and bedding to protect against the biting winter cold: such a blanket's warmth could mean the difference between survival and death in the harsh winters when sub-zero temperatures were common. They made these blankets by cutting hides spirally into continuous lengths and twisting them so that the fur side was out. After the skins had dried, they wove them together on a loom made of willow. It took about forty rabbit skins to make a child's robe, a hundred to make an adult man's robe.

The piñon nut harvest and the communal rabbit hunt were the only times the people gathered in larger groups, so these were also social events. The people had a year's events to catch up on: some of their friends had died; new children

had been born. Courtships blossomed as young men and women who had grown up in the year apart saw each other again. This was also a time to choose leaders, if necessary, and to resolve any problems between families. Only at such times were the people able to enjoy a sense of belonging to a larger group.

Once the snow began to fall in the mountains, the Great Basin Indians reluctantly said good-bye to their friends and separated into smaller family groups. It was easier to keep each person alive in a smaller group of people because game was even scarcer in the winter. They wintered in conical huts, which the men built of a domed willow framework and covered with any available material. Sometimes they laid down a layer of stones at the base to keep the supports firmly planted.

Many of the Basin people spent their winters in caves or sheltered canyons. Whether in a hut or a cave, they huddled around fires in their rabbit skin robes and lived on stores of rationed food:

dried fish, rabbit, jerky, piñon nut flour, dried berries, and seeds. The gray days of winter passed slowly: while men hunted for stray rabbits or birds, women pounded cedar bark and sagebrush into shreds that they could weave into clothing.

When ground squirrels began to emerge, followed by the returning migratory waterfowl, the people knew that winter was finally ending. Mallards and Canadian geese were welcome sights. Men made decoys to attract birds, and women waded into the chill marsh waters to collect edible tender shoots of the cattail.

Families left their winter shelters when the edible lowland greens ripened to collect the plants, seeds, and roots of spring. From spring through autumn was the Basin peoples' most intense period of searching for food; because no one place

## NORTHERN SHOSHONE POEM

I wonder who went to war
Leaving his little brother behind,
Standing alone.

Her brother went away,
She took his ring and kept it.
She cried when he left.
She heard her brother coming back.
His sister took the ring and came out.
Then he began to smile.

Wake up, wake up!
Start walking, friends!
I guess our sisters are sitting thinking.
Take rest for a day!

*A Wind River Shoshone man plays dice. Traditionally, gambling was a common and enjoyable way to pass leisure time.*

ever had sufficient resources to support a family for any period of time, they were constantly on the move.

In the dry areas, spring's warmth quickly dried up the meager resources, leaving only a few undependable water holes and small, brackish marshes. A family might discover that a stream that had seemed like a permanent water source

*A Paiute woman carries a burden basket with a tumpline on her head. Girls initially carried lighter loads; by the time they reached womanhood, they could carry heavily laden baskets.*

last year had become nothing more than a dry bed this year. But it was worth the search, because the tender roots of the cattail and tule came from these marshes. After the long and barren winter, green vegetables such as thistle, squaw cabbage, watercress, and clover tasted especially delicious. In the more southern deserts, the Indians also ate cactus.

In parts of the Great Basin where streams were located, the people were able to depend on fish. Salmon were so abundant in parts of Idaho that the Shoshone were able to establish villages where they could dry and store the fish. They also found ducks, geese, mud hens, grebe, and their eggs in the wetlands.

Late spring was a time for fishing at the mouths of rivers as schools of spawning fish began their upstream journey. The peoples of the Great Basin used spears to take spring trout, shiners, and suckers. The Paiute were especially fond of trout roasted over an open fire.

For the desert tribes, summer's simmering heat meant another season to be lived close to death. Temperatures often rose well above 100°F (38°C) in the desert. There was so little vegetation that the people there had to rely on insects—grasshoppers, ants, crickets, and caterpillars—for food. The grasshoppers may have seemed like a plague to the Mormon farmers who in 1847 arrived in what is now Utah, but for groups such as the Shoshone, the swarms that covered the countryside were a welcome treat and valued food source.

In the low foothills and valleys, seeds, rice grass, and berries ripened in the summer. Great Basin Indians used a seed beater or a wrapped stick to knock seeds loose from plants. The seeds were then carried in a twine basket to a residential camp, where they could be threshed with sticks and wooden paddles. After roasting the seeds, the people either ate them or stored them for winter.

By climbing nearby mountains, native peoples gained access to plants and animals from several climatic zones. Various seeds and berries (including elderberry, buffaloberry, chokecherry, currants, and serviceberry) ripened at different times. Elevation also affected ripening times. This meant that a particular kind of berry would be ripe in the valley while the same berry, higher up the mountain, ripened later, giving the people a longer period to gather and enjoy this valuable food.

In summer they also collected and dried other plants for winter storage, including edible bulbs, tubers, and roots such as camas, bitterroot, yampa, and sego. In what is now Yellowstone Park, the Indians collected over eighteen edible roots.

Once every eight to ten years the antelope population grew large enough for a communal antelope drive. The shamans of the Northern Paiute and Shoshone tribes performed ceremonies that featured songs intended to attract a herd of antelope. When the animals gathered, a circle of men surrounded and killed them. Just as the Plains Indians had uses for nearly every part of the bison, so the Great Basin Indians used the antelope, not only for food but also for clothing and bone tools, wasting no part of this valuable resource.

During the summer, Basin peoples lived in houses that were basically circular brush shelters built to provide relief from the sun. The Kawich Mountain Shoshone lived in wickiups—brush-covered, dome-shaped structures—in both summer and winter. For purification ceremonies, they built sweat lodges.

Some groups, including the Shoshone, eventually acquired horses from the Spanish by way of the Utes. Horses made their lives much easier by providing them access to a much wider territory in which to search for food. They were able to hunt bison in Wyoming, dry the meat, and carry it back to their homeland. The horse also made it possible to reach the salmon-rich streams of Idaho, and to search the Idaho prairies for camas bulbs.

Living on the edge of survival made the Indians of this region especially aware of their

## EATING CATERPILLARS

The Owens Valley Paiute, a Great Basin tribe, traditionally lived along the eastern slope of the southern Sierra Nevada Mountains in central California. The caterpillars of the pandora moth were part of their diet. They gathered the caterpillars, then roasted them in a pit under hot sand for an hour. After removing them from the pit, they sifted them with an open, plain-twine winnowing basket. The next step was to boil the caterpillars in water for an hour. Finally the caterpillars were ready to eat. Often they were dried and stored in a special shed, to be eaten later.

relationship with the Spirit Powers. Everything that existed had *puha,* or spiritual power. At times, puha was generous; at other times, puha did not seem to favor them.

The people realized that they were part of nature, not masters of it, and they always remembered to share what they had with all of creation, leaving something—a bead or a stone—in exchange for each root they dug from the earth. They said prayers of thanksgiving when they drank life-giving water from a stream and thanked the spirit of the mountain when they gathered piñon nuts from the trees that lined the mountain slopes.

*The Chemehuevi, a group of Southern Paiutes, covered a framework of horizontal and vertical poles with willow and arrowweed and often earth.*

# EUROPEAN CONTACT

In 1776, a Spanish expedition led by Silvestre de Escalante and Francisco Dominigues explored the southeastern part of the Great Basin. Thereafter, some Shoshone bands traded intermittently with the Spanish, but in general, there was little significant contact.

When prospectors rushed to California in search of gold in 1848, settlers followed close on their heels, disrupting 10,000 years of Great Basin life. In 1858, with the discovery of the Comstock Lode, Virginia City, Nevada, became a thriving urban center. The dust of wagon wheels soon blew away the Indians' fragile lifestyle, destroying the delicate balance that had allowed them to survive in the desert's cycles. The whites thoughtlessly leveled stands of piñon pines to have wood for fuel and let their horses and cattle trample the Indians' seed plots.

As happened each time whites came into contact with Indians, who lacked any immunity to the diseases of the white man, Indians died by the thousands. Two thousand Basin Indians died from cholera alone.

When the wagons kept coming and ranchers took more and more land, the peaceful Paiutes, who had never found glory in war, fled in panic. Many Western Shoshones and Utes hung around the fringes of white settlements, begging in order to survive. Occasionally they fought the whites, but they soon learned that it was futile to resist.

In 1863, the United States government consolidated the Indians on reservations, claiming the Great Basin without any formal treaty or payment.

*A young Paiute couple rides horses in the desert near Blanding, Utah. The board cradle on the woman's back has a shaped wooden framework with a fitted buckskin cover and an awning of twined willow to protect the baby.*

# ARTS AND CRAFTS

The peoples of the Great Basin spent most of their waking hours gathering food, which left them little time for art. Most of these groups made little pottery and basketry. Some of the Washo groups, however, who lived along the border between what is now California and Nevada, produced finely made baskets in addition to pitch-covered water jars and coiled plaques. Weaving by the Great Basin peoples was limited to rabbit fur blankets.

Today, the Washo, Paiute, and Shoshone on the Pyramid Lake Reservation at Dixon, Nevada, have created an arts and crafts cooperative called Wa-Pai-Shone Craftsmen. The Paiute in particular are known for their baskets and commercial glass bottles completely covered with beadwork. Tanned hides are another art form from this region.

The women of the Plateau region produced fine baskets. They used twining to make soft bags and hats, and coiling to create large storage containers. The Nez Percé, Umatilla, and Walla made flat twined wallets with multicolored designs. Other groups decorated their coiled baskets by sewing strips of colored grass or cherry bark onto the outer surface to create a surface of rectangular blocks with a technique called "imbrication." The Klikitat are especially known for their imbricated baskets, but the Yakima, Lillooet, Shuswap, Chilcotin, Thompson, and Fraser Indians also make these baskets.

Plains culture influenced the Plateau peoples to a large degree. When they developed a horse culture, they also adopted the beaded horse trappings—saddles, martingales, and cruppers—of the Plains peoples. As beads became available through trade, the Plateau peoples began to make the beaded skin clothing of the Plains tribes.

Today, some of the women on the reservations in the Plateau area continue to produce tribal arts and crafts. They use traditional styles and techniques to make contemporary pieces out of modern materials. Although the Nez Percé now use modern commercial yarns and jute string for their baskets, they still make them in the twined technique. Many Plateau peoples continue to exchange twined wallets or beaded bags filled with roots at inter-tribal gatherings. Some tribes still make fine imbricated baskets for sale. Horse trappings, clothing, and women's bags, decorated with fine beadwork, are always parts of inter-tribal powwows.

*Top: This Cayuse woman wears a twined basketry hat and a beaded buckskin dress and carries a Pendleton blanket. Left: Corn husk bags—flat, flexible wallets usually made of Indian hemp bast without a loom— are a well-known specialty of the Nez Percé. Parfleches, made of painted buffalo hide, were used for storage.*

## THE PLATEAU: A PATCHWORK OF CULTURES

*I wonder if everyone is up! It is morning. We are alive, so thanks be! Rise up! Look about! Go see the horses, lest a wolf has killed one! Thanks be that the children are alive!—and you, older men!—and you, older women!—also that your friends are perhaps alive in other camps.*

**—The speech shouted by the Herald of the Sun as he rode through the Nez Percé village each morning at dawn**

In contrast to the harshness of the Great Basin, where the people lived in constant fear of starvation, the Plateau was a land of abundance and great natural beauty. A typical Plateau culture was that of the band of Nez Percé led by Chief Joseph, who lived in the Wallowa Valley, surrounded by mountains covered by blue-green forests. Even in July, the crags of the Wallowa Mountains to the south still sparkled with snow. The valley floor, carpeted with bunchgrass and sage, was threaded by meandering streams where blueback salmon struggled upstream to spawn. The mirrored surface of Lake Wallowa was broken only by trout. The band's vast herds of ponies grazed peacefully; some Nez Percé chiefs boasted herds of two thousand or more horses in addition to their herds of

*White Bird, a Nez Percé, dressed in an elaborately beaded vest, cuffs, leggings, and moccasins. Such highly decorated Nez Percé dress developed after the introduction of the horse.*

*Eagle Calf, a Flathead chief, teaches Growing Good how to hold and aim his bow and arrow. Like other Plateau peoples, the Flathead adopted Plains dress.*

cattle. The Nez Percé, who had become respected horse breeders, carefully worked to improve the bloodlines of their herds. In their favorite trading place, the Grande Ronde River Valley, they exchanged their fresh ponies for those belonging to emigrants traveling the Oregon Trail; an Indian pony in good condition was worth several exhausted horses.

As with all Native American nations, the name that the whites applied to the Nez Percé is not the same as their own name for themselves. The French called these people Nez Percé ("pierced nose") because a few tribal members pierced their noses. The Nez Percé call themselves *Numípu,* which means "we people."

The peace-loving Nez Percé roamed the grassy plateaus and valleys during the spring, summer, and autumn. While their horses grazed, the men and boys hunted and fished. The women and girls gathered roots, berries, bulbs, and herbs, and made buckskin clothing and wove baskets and mats out of rushes. Each spring and autumn, the Nez Percé traveled across the Bitterroot Mountains to hunt buffalo on the eastern Montana plains, returning to their winter lodges in sheltered valleys before the cold winter storms moved into the region.

The Nez Percé were only one of many Plateau groups. This region is sometimes described as a patchwork quilt of cultures because the peoples of the Plateau reflected the cultural influences of their neighbors. This region is bordered by the Rocky Mountains on the east, the Cascade Range on the west, the upper reaches of the Fraser River on the north, and a line midway through what is now Oregon and Idaho on the south.

The Plateau enjoyed two great river systems— the Columbia and the Fraser. These rivers provided food—salmon—and served as avenues of travel and trade. Plateau groups traded with each other frequently, offering deerskin, Indian hemp for basketry, and bitterroot in exchange for valuable items from peoples who lived in surrounding regions. Over time, groups exchanged not only material goods but also cultural values.

Chinook merchants from the northwest came to the Plateau tribes, bringing sea otter pelts and decorated shells. After frequent contact with people of the Northwest Coast, the Klamath of the Plateau region adopted the Northwest Coast Indians' emphasis on achieving wealth and status. Some Plateau tribes even adopted the Northwest Coast practice of the potlatch, an elaborate giveaway that brought honor and status to the host. Several Plateau groups also borrowed concepts of personal beauty from some Northwest Coast tribes, including the customs of flattening heads by applying pressure bindings to an infant's head in the cradle board and of piercing noses.

Plateau peoples traded regularly with Plains tribes, as well. Plateau tribes such as the Nez Percé shared many Plains traits: they lived in tipis, wore feathered headdresses and beaded buckskin clothing, and were excellent horsemen. The Yakima, Nez Percé, Cayuse, and Palouse River Indians became known for their horse-breeding skills as they took full advantage of the well-watered grasslands of the Columbia River Basin where they lived. The Nez Percé, Coeur d'Alene, Shuswap, Thompson, and Lake Indians even adopted the Plains concept of counting coup as a way of winning personal honor in war.

*Flathead women could erect a tipi in a few minutes.*

# THE SANPOIL OF EASTERN WASHINGTON

The Sanpoil and their neighbors, the Nespelem, were central Plateau tribes that were less affected by outside influences. They did not borrow such Plains customs as horse breeding, and they probably lived closer to the original Plateau lifestyle. The Sanpoil hunted in forests but did not live there. About 1,600 Sanpoil lived in thirty villages located on both sides of the Columbia River in today's eastern Washington. The river played such a central role in their lives that the Sanpoil developed two types of canoe—a shallow dugout and a deeper, sharp-nosed canoe—which they used for trading, fishing, and visiting their relatives and friends.

The two principles governing Sanpoil life were pacifism and equality. The Sanpoil did not understand how the peoples of the Plains could take such delight in warfare or how their Northwest Coast neighbors could take slaves, live with a rigid system of social rankings, and care so much about the accumulation of wealth and status.

Both in villages and in individual families, the Sanpoil ideal was peace. They avoided all conflict: if one of their villages was attacked, the Sanpoil did not retaliate. The chief, whose main role was to be a peacemaker, reminded his people that war was futile and that no amount of fighting would bring back their dead loved ones or restore their property. Within families, maintaining peace was considered so important that in order to avoid tension and conflict, any member of the family was free to go to another village.

The Sanpoil also valued social and economic equality and shared their goods with each other. Even if a man did not participate in the activity of communal fishing, he still shared in the distribution of the catch.

These features of Sanpoil life—equality and the dislike of conflict—seem to be characteristic of the central Plateau peoples. The Sanpoil, in contrast to their Plains and Northwest Coast neighbors, had

*Sadie Boyd, a Nespelem woman, carries her baby in an elaborately beaded cradle board. Floral patterned beadwork is typical of the Plateau region.*

no strict rules of residence. When a couple married, they were not expected to live with either the bride or the groom's relatives; they could choose where they would live. They could settle in the wife's or the husband's home community, or they might choose to live in another community where they could make a better life for themselves. Individuals were free to leave a community at any time and to establish a new home in another village where they had distant relatives or no ties at all.

Like all Indians, the Plateau peoples structured their lives around the seasons. The Sanpoil weathered the severe winter by staying inside their houses and living on dried foods. Women passed

# THE UTE BEAR DANCE

*A line of women facing a line of men, with each woman dancing opposite the partner she has selected, forms the Bear Dance.*

Utes considered the bear a good hunter. In late winter, toward the end of February or the beginning of March, Ute bands performed the Bear Dance, to honor the bear. The dance was based on the story of the Ute hunter who saw a bear dancing outside a cave in the spring. The bear told the hunter that he would become a good hunter if he honored bears by performing the dance. The Utes also used this dance to publicly announce the completion of the female puberty ceremony.

---

the time by weaving baskets and mats and making deerskin clothing. The men gambled with dice and recounted stories.

To endure the endlessly cold, rainy months, they traveled to nearby villages for all-night get-togethers. The Sanpoil celebrated the winter solstice by gathering at communal houses to contact their guardian spirits. At these get-togethers, the people sang songs given to them by their guardian spirits, danced, gambled, and watched shamans perform thrilling feats such as assuming the spirits of grizzly bears. These ceremonies marked the midwinter point and made it easier to endure the rest of the long winter.

The severe winters of the Plateau region made clothing and housing important considerations. In the century before white contact, the Sanpoil adopted Plains-influenced buckskin clothing and moccasins. Before that, in summer men had worn a breechclout and the women an apron, both made of bark and deerskin. Men and women also wore woven ponchos. In winter they added leggings made of hemp for women and fur for men. Fur robes and blankets kept them warm. Before adopting Plains moccasins, they probably wore grass or skin foot coverings. The Sanpoil used porcupine quills to decorate their clothing.

The women used their prized mats of tule or slough grass as the basis of house construction as well as for bedding, berry drying, food preparation, and burials.

The Sanpoil built several kinds of dwellings, including semisubterranean earth lodges about 10 to 16 feet (3 to 4.8m) in diameter. Circular in shape, these structures each had a central pit and a conical or flat roof. In the center was a pole from which smaller poles radiated outward to the sides. The ceiling was made of planks or willow mats, and the roof was covered with layers of grass and brush, followed by a thick layer of earth. The entrance was through the roof, which they reached by means of a ladder.

In winter, the Sanpoil lived in an earth lodge or in a winter mat lodge that resembled an Iroquois longhouse, a communal dwelling with a length that varied depending upon how many families lived inside. A typical winter mat lodge was a gabled, tentlike structure measuring about 14 feet (4.2m) high, 16 feet (4.8m) wide, and from 24 to 60 feet (7.3 to 18.2m) in length. People entered through sets of double doors situated at both ends of the building. Insulated and rounded, similar to half a tipi, the entrance area provided a storm porch with two doors. Each person entered through the first door into a narrow, protected passage, and then passed through a second door to the living compartments. Inside, layers of mats and grass over a framework of poles provided more insulation from the cold winter wind and rain.

The summer houses were similar in shape to the winter homes except that each building housed just one family. Summer homes were either tipis covered with mats or circular windbreaks. The Sanpoil also set up summer fishing camps along the Columbia River, which featured rectangular, open-sided, flat-roofed structures. They placed these single-family dwellings end to end like the communal winter house. These houses were basically only windbreaks and might only be closed on one side. The Sanpoil hung fish to dry on the protected side of their fishing camp houses.

Everyone welcomed the activity and fresh food of spring: women gathered roots and prickly pear while men collected freshwater mollusks and hunted for rabbits and wildfowl. Everyone slept outside, delighting in their new freedom. The two mainstays of the Sanpoil diet were the men's salmon fishing and the women's root gathering. In late March the Sanpoil left their winter villages for the treeless plains south of the Columbia River, leaving in groups of four to five families until most of the village was gone. There, in the early spring, the women gathered a year's supply of roots. At the onset of the collecting, the people gave a ceremony of thanksgiving and shared the first harvest.

*Annie Johnson, a Nespelem woman from eastern Washington, sits with her children. She and her daughter wear traditional basketry hats.*

Their favorite of the edible roots, tubers, and stem plants that composed their diet was the camas root, which is a starchy bulb of the lily family. After the plant's petals withered, women dug out the bulb with willow digging sticks. They ate it raw or cooked it by roasting or pulverizing it into cakes that they boiled. The women also harvested the roots of the tiger lily, sunflower, cous, bitterroot, wild carrot, bracken fern, and dogtooth violet. Later in the year when berries ripened, the women made pemmican by pounding berries, fat, and venison together.

From early May through the end of October the men were busy fishing for the year's supply of fish, which would be stored and dried for winter. They began by catching enormous white sturgeon, which could weigh up to half a ton (0.4t). Later in the season, they caught trout and salmon.

The Sanpoil used a variety of methods for capturing fish: they not only speared and trapped fish but also dug shallow channels so that the fish would be easier to see. They built platforms as well, so that they could spear the fish below them in the channels. The men also used fishing weirs and willow traps.

While the men fished, the women set up their drying racks. They gathered the mounds of caught fish and began the ten- to fourteen-day process of drying the catch in the sun.

For most of the peoples in the Plateau region, salmon was a vitally important food source. The Sanpoil lived on the Columbia River and depended on four species of salmon as their primary food. A number of rituals and communal activities centered on the salmon. The Salmon Chief was responsible for supervising the First Salmon Ceremony, one of the most important group religious activities, as well as directing the actual fishing and the distribu-

tion of the catch. To become Salmon Chief, a man either had the salmon as one of his guardian spirits or was a shaman.

In September, some of the men took movable nets farther up- and downstream to catch more fish, in order to see the people through the long, cold winters. Women collected the last of the edible plants. Other men went hunting in groups for deer, elk, and antelope. They prepared for this hunt by participating in a sweat lodge ceremony so that their minds and bodies would be spiritually puri-fied and ready for the hunt.

By late October, the Sanpoil were snug in their winter camps. The men had repaired the roofs and gathered large piles of firewood, while the women had made new sleeping mats and insulated the house with fresh supplies of rye grass.

*Salmon fishing, as seen here on the Columbia River at Celio Falls, Oregon, provided the primary food for the peoples of the Plateau area.*

## EUROPEAN CONTACT

At first, the large-scale movement of the white man to the West Coast meant a greater variety of goods and profits for the trading tribes—the Klamath, Cayuse, Walla Walla, and Nez Percé—when they rendezvoused each summer. In 1775, when European vessels first docked at Nootka and Makah Indian settlements on the Northwest Coast, they brought steel knives, guns, and beads, which the Northwest Coast tribes traded to the peoples of the Plateau.

The Lewis and Clark Expedition, the first group of whites encountered by the Nez Percé, arrived in September—the month of the hunting moon—in 1805. They were amazed to find that the Indians had European-made knives. The Nez Percé gave the strange white people and the Shoshone woman, Sacajawea, who had guided them a big feast with an exchange of presents and a supply of camas root. When the expedition sailed down the great river to the ocean, they left their horses and saddles in the care of Chief Twisted Hair's Nez Percé band. Everything was returned to them in good condition the following spring when they returned.

In later years, after the Nez Percé had encountered more whites, they described Lewis and Clark as great men who did not wish to buy furs, to teach "spirit law," or to plow up Mother Earth for farms. Instead, they had come with a message of peace and friendship, which the Nez Percé cherished in their hearts.

The Plateau tribes enjoyed a short period of great prosperity after they acquired horses in the early 1800s. Lewis and Clark's descriptions of the rich Plateau area attracted trappers and traders to the area. Frontier trade blossomed, supplying the Indians with wonderful new things. The horse gave the Plateau tribes greater mobility so that groups such as the Nez Percé could travel to Sutter's Fort in California to trade with the Indians there. The Nez Percé were among the groups that adopted the richly decorated Plains horse gear and beaded shirts, leggings, and dresses.

### LIFE TODAY ON THE FLATHEAD RESERVATION

Today the Salish, Kootenai, and Pend d'Oreille tribes are known as the Confederated Salish and Kootenai Tribes. Their homeland once spread across 22 million acres (8.9 million ha) in northwestern Montana, northern Idaho, eastern Washington, and southwestern Canada. The Flathead Indian Reservation now includes about 1.2 million acres (0.4 million ha) of timber, farm, and grazing land.

The tribes are focusing on education and tribal development through a series of programs. The Flathead Nation is the largest employer in the area and owns and operates companies such as Flathead Post and Pole, Char-Koosta Printing (which produces a weekly newspaper), and S & K Electronics. They won the eventual right to purchase and manage Kerr Dam in 2015. This dam is one of the most valuable hydropower sites in the Pacific Northwest. In 1977, the tribes established Salish Kootenai College in Pablo. By 1991, the student body numbered over seven hundred Indians and non-Indians.

One of the most important aspects of their culture, the bison, has been restored. About four hundred American buffalo live on a large reserve with other animals in the National Bison Range at Moiese, Montana. Although the United States Fish and Wildlife Service manages this range, the tribes regulate camping, fishing, hunting, and other activities on the reservation.

However, white contact brought not only desired trade items and horses; it also brought disease and, eventually, displacement. Tragedy struck the Sanpoil when a group of their traders unknowingly carried back smallpox as well as trade goods to their people in 1782. The disease wiped out almost half their tribe before the end of the year.

Although both whites and Indians benefited from the early days of frontier trade, tensions increased as more Europeans arrived. Between 1829 and 1832, nearly all the Chinook Indians died from white diseases. Within a decade, land-hungry settlers were pouring into the rich farming land of Washington and Oregon, boxing in the peoples of the Plateau.

# SACAJAWEA

*Sacajawea guides the Lewis and Clark expedition over unfamiliar terrain.*

Sacajawea (1787–1812) was one of the most famous Indian women. Her exploits have captured the imagination of many people, and she is remembered in paintings and statues.

Sacajawea was a Shoshone whose people lived in the mountains near Three Forks, Montana. When she was about fourteen years old, however, she was captured by a Hidatsa war party who took her to their village in North Dakota. Toussaint Charbonneau, a French-Canadian fur trader who lived in the Hidatsa village, bought Sacajawea and arranged for his wife, who was also Shoshone, to care for her. About four years later, Charbonneau married Sacajawea as his second wife. In 1804, just after Charbonneau and Sacajawea's marriage, Lewis and Clark arrived with their expedition. They had been sent by President Jefferson to explore the country west of the Mississippi, which the United States had purchased from France the previous year, and to notify tribes in the new American territory that that they were now under the control of a new government.

Charbonneau was hired as a guide and interpreter, with the understanding that Sacajawea would also accompany the group. Lewis and Clark wanted her to guide the expedition when it reached Shoshone country so that she could speak to her people in their language and get their cooperation.

Soon after the Lewis and Clark expedition set out up the Missouri River with Sacajawea, she risked her life to save part of a boat's cargo. One of the most joyous moments of the trip came on July 22, when Sacajawea recognized her homeland. The next month she saw some of her people and began to dance for joy.

Sacajawea played a major role in the success of this expedition. Her intelligence, courage, and enthusiastic spirit won her the respect not only of Lewis and Clark but also of other whites with whom she came in contact. She was an extraordinary person who was able to see beyond the limits of her own life. It must have been difficult for her to once more leave her people and return to her life at a trading post. Sacajawea died in 1812, but she continues to live on as a vital part of American history.

Between 1843 and 1852, the Washington territorial governor, Isaac Stevens, bribed and threatened the remaining Plateau Indians into signing away their lands in fifty-two treaties. By concentrating the Indians on reservations, Stevens was able to acquire 157 million acres (63.8 million ha) of their land.

In 1842, the many bands of the Nez Percé nation met with Dr. Elijah White, subagent of Indian Affairs west of the Rocky Mountains. Dr. White suggested that they elect a head chief over all the Nez Percé bands; they chose a chief named Lawyer. Native Americans, including the Nez Percé, found the idea of rule by majority foreign and strange. Electing a single overall chief violated tribal custom, and the Indians did not fully understand the role of this leader. Traditionally, members of each band voluntarily followed the counsel and advice of their chief, who was assisted by minor chiefs and medicine men. Those who disagreed with their decisions remained band members but followed their own hearts.

The Yakima War of 1856–1858 began when hordes of disreputable white miners poured into Washington, leading to murders and reprisals. In 1857, the Indian Bureau sent J. Ross Browne to investigate. Browne told the Nez Percé chief Lawyer that the Treaty of 1855—which guaranteed certain lands for the Nez Percé—would be ratified by the Senate. However, army officials told the Indians that there was no way of knowing if the treaty would ever be signed. To complicate matters, Browne disobeyed his orders from the Indian Superintendent to tell the Indians that the Treaty of 1855 was inoperative until the Senate approved it. Chief Joseph expressed his frustration at the bureaucratic government of the United States:

> The white people have too many chiefs. They do not understand each other. They do not all talk alike....I cannot understand why so many chiefs are allowed to talk so many different ways, and promise so many different things.

In 1861, gold was discovered on the Lapwai Reservation in Idaho; between five and ten thousand

## SALISH KOOTENAI COMMUNITY COLLEGE

In 1976, the Confederated Salish and Kootenai Tribes founded the college on the Flathead Reservation in Montana. Estimates show that, compared to other Indian students, tribal college graduates are at least twice as likely to succeed in a non-Indian university. Tribal colleges also encourage Indian self-determination. One graduate of Salish Kootenai College heads the tribal forestry department. The supportive atmosphere encourages students: when a student has academic or absenteeism problems, instead of seeing this as an opening for a new student, two full-time staff members work with the student to keep him or her in school. Gerald Slater of Salish Kootenai College told the Carnegie Foundation:

*Many young people have a history of heavy drinking and have, in general, a lack of self-respect. But as they get more involved in traditional culture, they begin to get new self-respect—they will quit their drinking and begin to find a life that is more meaningful to them.*

Based on the principle that a firm cultural grounding develops a sense of self-worth, tribal colleges continue to grow in number.

miners converged there, disregarding every article of the 1855 treaty. For two years the government ignored Indian pleas to expel the whites as mining towns covered lands reserved for tipi villages.

Not only were the Indians subjected to abuses at the hands of the miners, who let nothing stand in their way, but the Indians also suffered from the poor administration of tribal affairs. Edward R. Geary, Superintendent of Indian Affairs for Oregon, reported that supplies for the reservations routinely arrived

> ...damaged in transportation. Had one half of the amount laid out in these purchases been expended in opening farms on the reservation, and the buying of stock cattle and sheep, it would have inured vastly to the benefit of the Indians.

# CHIEF JOSEPH

*Chief Joseph, statesman and reluctant warrior.*

O ur fathers gave us many laws, which they had learned from their fathers. These laws were good. They told us to treat all men as they treated us; that we should never be the first to break a bargain; that it was a disgrace to tell a lie; that we should speak only the truth; that it was a shame for one man to take from another his wife, or his property without paying for it. We were taught to believe that the Great Spirit sees and hears everything.

Chief Joseph (1840–1904), chief, warrior, and diplomat, was one of the most strategic Indian leaders in the fight against the United States Army. His Indian name was Thunder-rolling-in-the-mountains, a name that offered the protection of nature, a perfect name for one who led his people so valiantly.

For the freedom of his people, he led his three hundred warriors against veteran troops, fresh from their Civil War victory at Appomattox. Although Chief Joseph was not the "war chief," he fought in self-defense, serving as the camp guard of the women, children, and old men. For thirty-three years—from 1871 to 1904—Joseph used every possible resource to win justice for his tribe. After exhausting every peaceful means, including noncooperation, he unwillingly resorted to fighting. Even then he adhered to the white man's civilized code of war, forbidding his warriors to commit any atrocities.

Brigadier General Oliver O. Howard, hero of the Civil War battles at Antietam and Gettysburg, fought against Joseph, declaring him to be a remarkable leader: "No general could have planned a battle more skillfully."

Although Chief Joseph died in exile in 1904, he was reburied in his beloved Wallowa homeland less than a year later. In 1879, he had described this area as "that beautiful valley of winding waters. I love that land more than the rest of the world."

In 1862, the federal government cut off supplies to the reservation and diverted more resources to waging the Civil War. In 1863, the government appointed a commission to negotiate a new treaty to calm the Indians, who were frustrated and furious at the government's inability to live up to the agreement. In addition to the government's failure to send much-needed supplies and the unlivable conditions on the reservation, miners, traders, farmers, and stockmen completely disregarded reservation boundaries. White men took Indian women to live with them, then deserted the women, leaving the starving tribe to support their children. Furthermore, Southern sympathizers among the miners spread rumors about the collapse of the federal government.

The Nez Percé were more profoundly attached to the land than were other tribes because of Smohalla's Earth-Mother or Dreamer religion—similar to the Ghost Dance—and also because they returned each year to the deeply cherished homeland of their fathers.

This love of home eventually caused the Nez Percé nation to split: the federation dissolved because some of the head chiefs refused to cede their treasured land, which included Chief Joseph's beloved Wallowa Valley, to the whites. This termination of the federation meant that Chief Lawyer was no longer authorized to speak for the bands that had left the federation, but the United States government still considered his signature on the treaty to be binding to all bands of the Nez Percé nation.

Chief Joseph used an allegory to explain why Lawyer had no authority to sign away the Wallowa (Winding Water) Valley in Oregon, which had always been the territory of Joseph's father's people:

> Suppose a white man should come to me and say, "Joseph, I like your horses, and I want to buy them." I say to him, "No, my horses suit me, I will not sell them." Then he goes to my neighbor, and says to him: "Joseph has some good horses. I want to buy them, but he refuses to sell." My neighbor answers, "Pay me the money, and I will sell you Joseph's horses." The white man returns to me, and says, "Joseph, I have bought your horses, and you must let me have them." If we sold our lands to the Government, this is the way they were bought.

Eventually, aggressive white movement into the Plateau area led to the 1877 Nez Percé war. After having been bullied into signing 374 land-reducing treaties, the Nez Percé were finally given thirty days to depart their homeland. When several Nez Percé horses were stolen, the younger warriors lost their patience and killed eighteen settlers, sparking a series of violent conflicts with the United States Army. Ultimately, under the leadership of Chief Joseph, the Nez Percé undertook a 1,600-mile (2,560km) flight toward Canada. Troops captured the Nez Percé only 30 miles (48km) from the Canadian border. Despairing, Chief Joseph made the eloquent surrender speech that begins this chapter.

## CHIEF JOSEPH'S HOMELAND TODAY

*An Appaloosa galloping across Chief Joseph's ancestral lands. Once held in vast herds, only a few of these horses remain to the Nez Percé.*

The homeland of Chief Joseph's band of Nez Percé is a land of high plains, rolling hills, deep canyons, and forest-encircled lakes. The present-day town of Joseph, Oregon, is in the northeastern part of the state between the Grande Ronde and Imnaha Rivers. Every year, during the final weekend of July, the town hosts Chief Joseph Days, and members of Chief Joseph's Wallowa band of Nez Percé travel from the Colville Reservation in Washington to this non-Indian community.

The Nez Percé formed a Cultural Resources Program in 1988 in an effort to preserve their language, history, and arts. They are developing a language curriculum program for Nez Percé schoolchildren. The Nez Percé were famous for their great herds of Appaloosas, but when the tribe surrendered to Colonel Nelson Miles in 1877, they had to give up their 1,100 horses. In 1991, Bob Browning, a New Mexico Appaloosa breeder, donated ten of his mares to the nonprofit, tribally-sponsored Chief Joseph Foundation, which is using them to promote cultural pride.

# CHAPTER FIVE

# >THE<
# NORTHWEST
# COAST

*Even the rocks that seem to lie dumb as they swelter in the sun along the silent seashore in solemn grandeur thrill with memories of past events connected with the fate of my people, and the very dust under your feet responds more lovingly to our footsteps than to yours, because it is the ashes of our ancestors, and our bare feet are conscious of the sympathetic touch, for the soil is rich with the life of our kindred.*

—Chief Seattle's speech
to the governor of Washington Territory, 1854

# LANGUAGES OF THE TRIBES OF THE NORTHWEST COAST

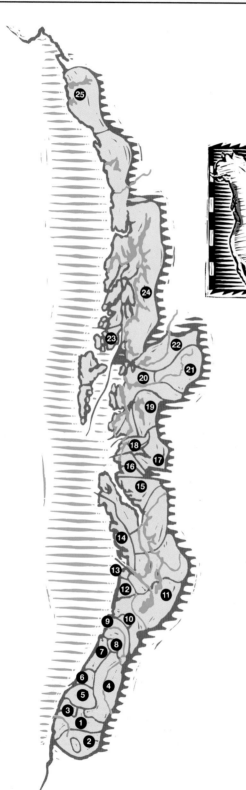

| | | | |
|---|---|---|---|
| 1. | Athabascan | 14. | Nootka |
| 2. | Takelma | 15. | Kwakiutl |
| 3. | Coos | 16. | Oowekeeno |
| 4. | Kalapuyan | 17. | Bella Coola |
| 5. | Siuslawan | 18. | Bella |
| 6. | Alsean | 19. | Haisla |
| 7. | Tillamook | 20. | Tsimshian |
| 8. | Clatskanie | 21. | Gitksan |
| 9. | Chinook | 22. | Nishga |
| 10. | Kwalhioqua | 23. | Haida |
| 11. | Salish | 24. | Tlingit |
| 12. | Quileute | 25. | Eyak |
| 13. | Makah | | |

*Except for the natives of California, the Indians of the Northwest Coast used a greater variety of languages than the peoples of any other region. They spoke at least forty-five different languages but shared a common culture.*

*In the Algonquian (Wakashan) family, there were the Nootka, Kwakiutl, Squamish, Nisqualli, Cowlitz, Tillamook, Bella Coola, and Salish. The Penutian family is represented by the Chinook people. In the Nadene (Athabascan) family of languages, there were such tribes as the Haida, Eyak, and Tlingit. Some linguists consider Tlingit and Haida to be language isolates, which means that these languages do not belong to any language family. Each of these language families can be further divided into branches and then into distinct languages. Different groups spoke their own dialect of the same language. While dialects are mutually intelligible, different languages are not. (For example, in North America we speak many dialects of English; if a Texan speaks clearly enough, a New Yorker can understand him or her and vice versa.)*

The tribes of the Northwest Coast developed some of the most sophisticated and artistic cultures in North America. Unlike most of the native peoples of this part of the continent, the Indians of this area had little or no contact with the strong cultural influence  from the territory of present-day Mexico. In addition, the culture of the Northwest Coast tribes was so unique and vigorous that it influenced some of the Plateau and California tribes.

The Northwest Coast region is the long, narrow arc of land that extends along the North Pacific coast of North America from the Gulf of Alaska to the mouth of the Chetco River on the southern Oregon Coast. Because the mountains are so close to the sea, the inland boundary of the Northwest Coast—which follows the crests of mountain ranges—never penetrates the interior more than 200 miles (320km), and in many places, it is much closer to the coast. Wisely choosing to settle near beaches, fjords, and the mouths of rivers, and on off-coast islands, the peoples of this region had access to abundant sea resources.

A visitor to a Northwest Coast village would have immediately seen the people's dependence on the sea and on the forest, from the chimney-high totem poles that towered over immense cedar houses to the carved canoes and smoke racks for drying fish. Nearly every village—whether it housed fifty or one thousand people—faced the water, be it the ocean or a stream, and nearly everything in a village—houses, totem poles, canoes—was made of wood. While the peoples of the Great Basin struggled merely to survive, the Northwest Coast peoples lived in a land of such abundance that they could amass a year's food

*Top: Skokomish Indians in their cedar canoes. The summer fishing shelter behind them is covered with mats. Above: Nootkas roast fish in a cooking box while more fish dry on overhead racks normally used for winter storage. Sleeping platforms line the plank walls of this multifamily dwelling. The man at left is wearing a woven spruce-root hat.*

supply in several months, from mid-May to mid-September. The ocean and rivers teemed with life—salmon, halibut, trout, whales, sea lions. The deeply wooded mountains that rose sharply behind their villages provided elk, bear, mountain goat, and deer.

The Indians never took the bounty of their surroundings for granted. Appreciative of every resource, they taught respect for all living things and performed rituals of thanksgiving for everything they used. For example, they considered the life-giving salmon to be a race of immortals who wintered in deep sea dwellings. In late spring the Salmon-Men assumed the form of fish and swam upstream to give up their lives for humans. But because the Salmon-Men were immortal, if fishermen returned their bones to the rivers after stripping their flesh, the bones would be reborn as men when they reached the ocean. And the life-giving cycle of the Salmon-Men would continue.

The people also honored the spirit of the salmon by performing a ritual of thanksgiving over the first salmon caught each spring, much as the farming Indians of previous chapters performed rituals over the first fruits of their harvest. This first fish was considered to be the leader of the Salmon-Men. A holy man, who knew the appropriate prayers, respectfully carried the salmon to an altar, where he sprinkled the salmon with red ocher or sacred eagle down and said prayers. After the fish had been cooked, everyone tasted of this first, honored salmon. Only after the salmon had been treated to a ceremony of reverence could the fishing begin.

Images of salmon often appear in Northwest Coast art because of the fish's importance in their life. The Nootka people of Vancouver Island's west coast made a ceremonial mask carved of red cedar

*Above: The spirit of the sun comes alive in this Bella Coola mask. Left: Makah Indians bake salmon at Neah Bay, Washington. The salmon was the basis for the abundant economy of Northwest Coast peoples because the salmon's life cycle made bountiful catches predictable events.*

depicting seven salmon to acknowledge the superhuman power that brought the salmon to the Nootka.

Although no fish was as important to the people as the salmon, they also caught other species, including herring and smelt. They were especially fond of the eulachon, or candlefish, both for its delicious flesh and its fine oil, which they used for cooking, seasoning, and medicine. Because the peoples of the Northwest Coast depended upon the resources of the sea for sustenance, they developed an incredibly complex set of tools for fishing, including special implements and methods for the capture of each kind of fish.

For taking salmon, the people built weirs—wooden fence-like enclosures that spanned the river—to keep the salmon from swimming upstream. Once the salmon came through the weir's

*Northwest Coast Indians carved monumental human, animal, and mythic creatures from cedar wood.*

gates, the men used 16-foot (4.8m) harpoons to spear the fish. They also used dip nets—wooden frameworks hung with netted bags—to catch the fish. Latticework traps shaped into boxes and cylinders were even more efficient in capturing the struggling salmon as they fought their way upstream.

To hook halibut and cod, the men climbed into their great ocean-going canoes and headed seaward. Some Northwest Coast groups, like the Nootka, even caught whales, while others sought sea otter and seals. These fish and sea mammals supplied welcome variety in their diet. To catch salmon in deep saltwater, the people used barbed hooks; for northern halibut they used a piece of cedar or yew bent into a U-shaped hook with a horn barb or lashed bone baited with octopus. Once the fisher-

men caught a halibut, which could weigh 200 pounds (90.8kg) or more, they pulled it in along the side of the canoe and killed it with a club specially designed for this purpose. They had an array of smaller hooks for snagging dogfish, cod, and herring. They also used seines, dip nets, rakes, and open-mesh baskets to catch herring.

The heavy rains and mild climate of the Northwest Coast produced unusually abundant vegetation. The dark, deeply wooded mountains that rose behind the narrow beaches provided game and plants for food and housing. In addition to the deer, elk, bear, wolf, mountain goat, otter, marten, and beaver, there were edible plants such as wild celery, roots, and berries.

The forest's main bounty, however, were the red and yellow cedars, huge trees that the people felled with bone and stone drills, hardwood wedges, and stone tools. The magnificent forests of the lush Northwest Coast provided timber for canoes, housing, weapons, tools, containers, and totem poles. As a result, the peoples of this region were probably the most accomplished woodworkers in North America.

After felling the trees they had selected, the people often rolled the massive logs to the water to let the current transport them to their villages. After storms they looked for felled trees, which they used for house construction. They also used cedar bark to make baskets, clothing, whaling ropes, and canoes.

The peoples of the Northwest Coast used canoes as their basic method of transportation. The Tlingit,

# CANOE BUILDING TODAY

*This Bella carver paints the prow of a canoe. In recent years, the art of canoe building has been reborn among the peoples of the Northwest Coast.*

Northwest Coast legends tell how, long ago, the ancestral Cedar Tree gave dugout cedar canoes to the Cedar People. For the tribes of the Northwest Coast, the canoe was an essential part of life—used for fishing, travel, trading, potlatches, sport, and war. Sadly, by 1985, these Indians had almost lost the art of canoe making, and most of their canoes were in museums.

Emmett Oliver, a seventy-two-year-old Quinault Indian, however, had other ideas. When the Maritime Committee of the Washington State Centennial Commission asked him to arrange a Native American event, he envisioned tribally carved canoes paddling across Puget Sound to Seattle, followed by two days of canoe racing.

Oliver had many obstacles to overcome. Some tribes did not want to participate in the state's one hundredth birthday celebration when the entire state had been theirs until Europeans began arriving. But Oliver explained that this was an opportunity to bring back the canoe, a vitally important part of their culture and way of life.

The tribes also had to get permission from the government to fell some six-hundred-year-old cedar trees, which were protected by law. Because canoes are such a significant part of Native American spiritual life, permission was granted under the 1978 Religious Freedom Act. Each tribe was allowed to fell two of the enormous 5-foot (1.5m) -diameter, 70-foot (21.3m)-high cedars. Before the people began to cut each tree, women

said prayers and sang blessing and thanksgiving songs. They thanked the tree for giving its life, explaining that it would be reborn as a canoe.

As work progressed on the canoes, the people prepared themselves spiritually. The Quileute on the Pacific at La Push taught canoe carving and paddling in their schools. The paddlers purified themselves, avoiding drugs and alcohol. To paddle a canoe, a person had to be both spiritually and physically fit. The task of canoe carving also required spiritual awareness, and the carvers sought guidance from the spirits of the trees.

On June 10, 1989, at their First Salmon Ceremony, the Tulalip launched a 25-foot (7.6m) canoe. The Port Gamble Klallam launched their 35-foot (10.6m) canoe later that month.

In July the Quileute, Klallam, and Lower Elwha sailed their canoes to Hadlock, south of Port Townsend. There on the beach, they joined together for a salmon feast with tribal songs, dances, and stories. On this ancient potlatch site, used for centuries by their ancestors, they renewed their culture and their hope.

Some twenty tribes and forty canoes assembled on July 20, 1989, at Suquamish, the site of Chief Seattle's longhouse. This was the rendezvous point for crossing Puget Sound to Seattle. That night, some seven hundred people gathered for a salmon and clam bake. Again, there were spectacular performances with traditionally dressed dancers, singers, and drummers.

The next morning they crossed the starting line to Seattle. When they reached Shilshole Bay, five thousand people greeted them. In the evening, the Duwamish hosts fed more than a thousand people. Tribal dances, stories, and songs followed the canoe races. Saturday there were more races. Frank Brown, of the Bella Heiltsuk, expressed the spirit of the occasion well when he told *Native Peoples* magazine, "To lose a ceremony is to lose the past; to create a ceremony is to create the future."

who lived on the mainland and islands of the southeastern Alaska panhandle; the Haida, of the Queen Charlotte Islands in British Columbia; and the Tsimshian, who lived on the mainland and coastal islands of northwestern British Columbia, were all masters of canoe building. Some of them made as many as seven different types of canoes, with the war/ceremonial canoe as the most impressive.

To make a ceremonial canoe, a Haida craftsman began with a 60- to 70-foot (18.2 to 21.3m) red cedar log split lengthwise. Using an adze, he shaped the bottom and the sides of the canoe, then hollowed out the inside of the vessel. The next step was to soften the wood by partially filling the dugout log with water heated by hot stones, while a nearby fire heated the exterior of the canoe. This allowed him to widen the canoe by pushing the softened sides of the dugout farther apart with a series of posts. The canoe maker then added a projected bow, attached to the hull with ropes of cedar, to repel wave action in stormy seas, improving the canoe's stability. He also attached a stern piece. Finally, he placed cedarwood gunwales along the sides of the canoe. After the canoe was sanded and polished, the canoe owner added a carved figure,

> ## HAIDA SONG FOR FINE WEATHER
>
> O good Sun,
> Look thou down upon us:
> Shine, shine on us, O Sun,
> Gather up the clouds, wet, black, under thy arms—
> That the rains may cease to fall.
> Because their friends are all here on the beach
> Ready to go fishing—
> Ready for the hunt.
> Therefore look kindly on us, O Good Sun!
> Give us peace within our tribe
> And with all our enemies.
> Again, again, we call—
> Hear us, hear us, O Good Sun!

such as a wolf, at the bow and painted his crests on the side of the craft. He might also have added inlays to highlight the effect of the painted crests.

Sometimes, the Haida lashed two canoes together, laying a plank deck over them, like the Polynesians, although they did not use these crafts to sail the ocean.

*A Kwakiutl carver stands behind an immense serving vessel that is in the form of a human figure lying on its back. Such enormous serving vessels were associated with the feasting that was part of every potlatch. During the twelve days of the potlatch, the host honored his guests by supplying more fish, meat, berries, and fish oil than the hundreds of guests could eat while guests showed their gratitude by consuming as much as humanly possible.*

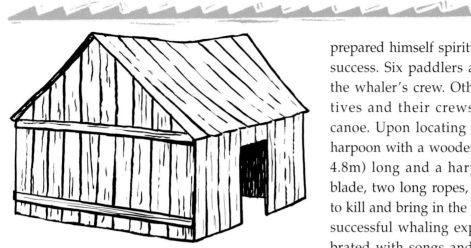

*The Haida winter house provided shelter for about six related families.*

The Nootka, who lived on Vancouver Island, ventured into the open seas between March and August in search of California gray whales, humpback whales, and possibly right whales. They considered whaling to be the noblest of all occupations. The whaler was always a chief who prepared himself spiritually for months to ensure success. Six paddlers and a steersman made up the whaler's crew. Other canoes led by his relatives and their crews accompanied the main canoe. Upon locating a whale, the chief used a harpoon with a wooden shaft 14 to 16 feet (4.2 to 4.8m) long and a harpoon head armed with a blade, two long ropes, lances, and sealskin floats to kill and bring in the enormous creature. After a successful whaling expedition, the Nootka celebrated with songs and prayers of thanksgiving, thanking the spirit of the whale for its sacrifice of life so that the Nootka could live.

The peoples of the Northwest Coast built massive houses that were even more impressive than their canoes. These permanent multifamily homes were built for stability and status. They measured at least 40 feet (12.1m) long and 30 feet (9.1m) wide. The groups of the north built their homes from yel-

*American painter Arthur Jansson depicted these Northwest Coast Indians fishing and cooking their catch. On the river behind them is an ornately carved canoe.*

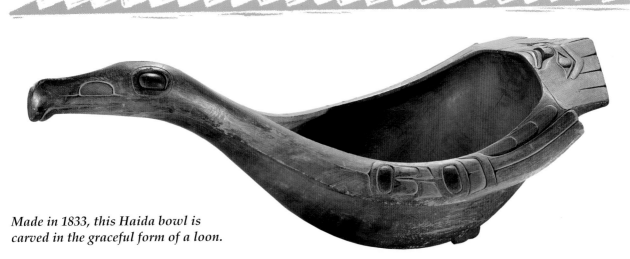

*Made in 1833, this Haida bowl is carved in the graceful form of a loon.*

low cedar, while the central and southern Northwest Coast peoples used red cedar.

After selecting and clearing the site chosen for a new house, the builders chose the perfect logs, felled the trees, and split them into planks and beams. After preparing the boards, the builders put up a framework of large upright beams and long ridgepoles that ran lengthwise, supported by a post on either end. They then mortised the frame work together securely. The building was weather proof because the roof and the sides were built of overlapped planking. The only exterior light came through a ventilation hole in the roof that could be covered when it rained.

Many Northwest Coast peoples often built their houses partly underground. Haida chiefs had several tiers of benches extending from a central pit—rather like a sunken living room—upward to ground level. Rank determined the position of families' living quarters within the house, with the family of the highest ranking resident living in a place of honor along the back wall. Other families lived in apartments arranged according to rank.

The impressive architecture of the Northwest Coast tribes was a sign of wealth—houses like these required considerable outlay of resources. After the owner had enough time to amass more wealth, he often added an elaborately carved and expensive totem pole.

Sometimes, a single house was a village in itself, while a dozen or so houses could be found in other villages. The people of a village had to decide if they had enough available resources and manpower to build more houses. On the other hand, they might need to invest in better defense against warring tribes. They might also choose to spend their resources in the display of status by sponsoring a potlatch, an expensive ceremony that took the form of a party hosted by a family who gave gifts to all the guests.

Northwest Coast peoples also used wood as the material for everyday dishes, spoons, and ladles; sometimes they used mountain sheep horns to make utensils. For ceremonial feasts, they carved elaborate wooden troughs and bowls. With only limited tools—wooden wedges, bone drills, and stone adzes, chisels, and carving knives—the people of the Northwest created magnificently crafted structures and objects. After they acquired metal tools from the whites, they were able to carve bowls of slate and steatite.

The peoples of the Northwest Coast made and displayed several kinds of carved poles, including a memorial pole that was erected by the heir of a chief when he assumed the chief's rank, and a mortuary post, which was placed by a chief's grave. The most dramatic carvings were found on the doorway house posts, which were often 37 feet (11.2m) high and depicted fantastic, elaborately carved symbolic animals whose forms flowed into one another. A typical house post might have at its base Dogfish with Killerwhale in its mouth, Thunderbird, Raven, and Sea Grizzly Bear, with

## TOTEM POLES

*Above: Stately totem poles frame the Haida village of Skidegate on the Queen Charlotte Islands. The Haida were especially adept at carving. Right: Thunderbird, Sea Grizzly Bear, Raven, and three watcher guardians decorate the 37-foot (11.2m) -high house post.*

The totem pole has become the symbol for the Northwest Coast. Instead of totems, however, these figures are more properly called crests. Totems required special behavior; for example, if a clan had the bear as their totem, clan members had to follow special taboos or restrictions regarding bears. The animals represented on these poles, however, were not totems, but rather helping spirits related to the special guardian spirit of the clan ancestor. The carved figures were more like a visual family tree of ancestors. Contrary to the beliefs of the early missionaries, who destroyed many of the most impressively carved poles, these figures were not worshiped.

three human watchmen-guardians in potlatch hats sitting at the very top. These hats were woven and decorated with rings—for each potlatch the owner of the house gave, another ring could be added.

Such doorway house-posts were a form of totem pole. Totem poles, which depicted certain animals, birds, fish, heavenly bodies, and prominent landmarks, symbolically recorded the glories of the house owner's ancestors. Totems were much more than just emblems or beautiful designs; they were spiritual guides. Northwest Coast peoples addressed the actual animals, mountains, glaciers, and even dangerous bodies of water as "uncles" and "aunts." The spirit of that being then responded by helping the person who had called upon it. People whose clan had a special relationship with the bear, for example, were great bear hunters. Although totems played an essential role in the spiritual world of Northwest Coast peoples, they did not worship their totems.

Tlingit mothers honored their clan ancestors so profoundly that they even named their children after them, enabling the spirit of the deceased ancestor to be reborn in the child through the name. When she was ready to give birth, a pregnant woman went to a bark shelter intended for birthing, where she remained for ten days after her child was born.

When a Tlingit boy was about eight years old, he went to live with his mother's brother, whose task was to teach the boy discipline. The boy learned to respect and obey his uncle, even when the lessons required such unpleasant acts as plunging into icy water to purify himself. The boy's uncle also taught him practical tasks, such as chopping wood, and important skills, including hunting rituals, as well as tribal history. The boy listened closely when his uncle recounted the traditions of his clan and lineage, especially since if the uncle had no other heirs, the boy would inherit his uncle's house and position.

Girls had their own lessons to learn. The most important event of a girl's life was the onset of menstruation; her behavior during this experience determined not only her future but also that of her relatives. She spent this time in a menstruation hut, where the length of her confinement depended upon her father's wealth and her rank. As she fasted for several days, she learned about clan traditions from her father's sister, her mother, or her maternal grandmother. She also practiced adult skills like basketry. When she rejoined the village, her relatives bathed her, gave her new clothes, and pierced her lip for an ornament. At a potlatch ceremony given by her father's sisters, the girl was presented as a woman ready for marriage.

The Tlingit, in all their villages, divided the people into two hereditary groups called moieties. The two moieties were the Ravens and the Wolves (also called the Eagles). Each person belonged a clan within the Raven or Wolf group and to a lineage within his or her clan. Each lineage often occupied a single house. A person belonged to the lineage, clan, and group of his or her mother, and had to marry a person of the opposite group: thus, a Raven could not marry another Raven.

During adolescence, children learned the family history, including the exploits, victories, wealth, and honorable history of the clan. The house chief often gathered the children together around the fire pit on damp, chilly winter evenings to tell them clan stories and history.

Families arranged marriages to strengthen clan relationships and to bring greater wealth to the families. Families often began to arrange a girl's marriage while she was in seclusion during her first menstruation.

*A Tlingit woman wears a button blanket. Made of flannel, the blanket is outlined with hundreds of small iridescent buttons, each sewn on with sinew. Such blankets could have as many as three thousand buttons.*

Gift-giving and an elaborate show of wealth played a big part in a Tlingit marriage. The couple received gifts, as did both families. The number of gifts exchanged between the families reflected the generosity of the givers, giving them greater status. The bride was married at her father's home.

Rank was also important in Tlingit death rites; although mourning ceremonies were similar for men, women, and children, they were most elaborate for a man of high rank. When such a man died, often at the end of a long and fruitful life after many successful potlatches, his body would lie in state for four days. He was dressed in his ceremonial clothes and the traditional clan design was painted on his face. The treasures of his lineage were piled beside him. The men of the opposite moiety carried the body through an opening in the

*A Tlingit medicine man sits with his two wives. Polygamy was practiced occasionally among Northwest Coast tribes.*

wall made by removing a wall plank. (Many Indian societies throughout northern North America believed that the dead should not leave the home through the same door that was used by the living.) The body was then cremated.

The peoples of the Northwest Coast possessed a rich oral tradition for expressing themselves, and for explaining the nature of the world and the importance of fundamental values. In the autumn and winter, after they had finished the autumn fishing and had packed away stores of dried fish and berries, the men and women left their summer camps and moved back to their permanent villages. The time of the great ceremonies and nights of storytelling was about to begin.

As with all Native Americans, the peoples of the Northwest Coast lived in constant awareness of the spirits around them: those of the deep, impenetrable forests—Bear, Wolf, and the impulsive trickster Raven—and those of the powerful, surging ocean—Whale, Sea Otter, and the immortal Salmon-Men. The people used their dreams, visions, and traditional knowledge to reproduce ancient images of the

spiritual beings. They created elaborate ceremonial masks used in telling the stories of the spirits.

Many of these tales stemmed from days long past, when the boundaries between the worlds of humans, animals, and spirits were less defined. Raven, the gluttonous trickster-transformer, played a central role in the creation stories of the Tlingit, Haida, and Tsimshian. Neither good nor evil, Raven was a compelling symbol of change. His actions created many of the features of the existing world. He usually brought about change in the world through his selfishness, which nevertheless often had beneficial side effects for the human race.

Each mask maker put a part of himself into his carving as he fashioned images that were powerful because of the forces they represented. Borrowing colors and forms from the living universe around him, talking to the image as he worked, he created his own unique vision. Even masks that portrayed the same spirit were not completely alike because each maker presented his own interpretation of the story connected with the figure. The mask wearer told the story during a ceremony in the dramatic light of the campfire. (Only rarely did the wearer tell the full tale, for such knowledge was powerful and it was dangerous and wrong to give away all of one's power.) Deep shadows filled the corners of the immense cedar longhouse as a steady downpour of cold rain made everyone glad to be inside with their family and friends.

Fantastic creatures with snapping jaws and movable fins and tails danced beside the flames: a human figure astride a raven sat on the forehead of a man, the spirit of the life-giving sun in all its glory. A favorite mask depicted the spirit of Echo in his many guises. This creature, who could imitate the sounds made by any being, was represented by a mask with interchangeable mouths; the wearer hid his face beneath the folds of his blanket to replace Echo's mouth with the mouth of the creature—a human being, Beaver, Eagle, Bear, or Raven—that Echo was imitating during each part of the story. The sea urchin mask split open to reveal another image, used in the course of storytelling as the original creature revealed its inner being.

A particularly important person in Northwest Coast spiritual life was the shaman, a respected individual who inspired great awe for his abilities to cure, to influence the weather, to assure an abundant salmon harvest, to predict the future, to find witches, and to bring victory in war. Both female and male shamans served an apprenticeship with an older shaman but derived their powers from their personal guardian spirits whom they encountered during a period of solitary fasting. A shaman also healed people, interceding with the spirits on behalf of his or her patient.

Northwest Coast religious ceremonies often featured secret societies that performed complicated sacred rituals. One of the most interesting was the Kwakiutl Shaman's Society, of which the highest ranking shaman was the Hamatsa, or Cannibal Dancer. Because the Kwakiutl avoided contact with the dead, the idea of eating human flesh was awful and awe-inspiring to them. Through annual ceremonials, the Hamatsas impressed nonmembers with their power through drama and magic. The dancers' bodies were supposedly taken over by the cannibal spirits, which led them to leap about in a frenzy as they screamed and pretended to eat human flesh. Accompanying rites pacified the cannibal spirits. During this carefully staged presentation, hidden attendants made carved birds swoop over the audience and strange voices howl from the floorboards. The dancers vanished in puffs of smoke.

*Top: A Haida transformation mask portrays a man who becomes a woman. Above: A carved wooden raven rattle used by a Tlingit shaman to call up his guardian spirit.*

# POTLATCHES AND SLAVES

The potlatch—a Chinook word meaning "to give"—was a massive feast given by the house of one clan to honor the house of another clan. By dispensing food and gifts lavishly, the hosts of the potlatch displayed their wealth and confirmed their status. Often the lineage group worked together, amassing the wealth that was to be given away to another lineage. Sharing this important group activity gave everyone a sense of belonging. The potlatch established continuing good relations with another lineage because the gifts were given by one group and received by the other—people did not potlatch the members of their own family.

Among the Northwest Coast peoples, rank and privilege were inherited. Nevertheless, a person had to earn enough wealth to validate this inherited position; upon giving a potlatch he or she would be recognized by others. By giving gifts, the host of the potlatch sought public acknowledgment of his status. By accepting the gifts, guests agreed that the host, or a member of his family, had the right to take on a privileged title inherited from his or her lineage.

It took years to prepare for a potlatch, partly because it took so long to amass the gifts. Throughout the days of the potlatch, guests were showered with gifts: each of the several hundred guests received a present, ranging from cedar bark blan-

*These clan members are the honored guests of another Tlingit clan at a potlatch. Their hosts will display their wealth by generously providing guests with food and gifts.*

## ARTS AND CRAFTS

The main material of Northwest Coast art was, and is, wood. The peoples of this region made beautifully decorated wooden storage boxes, food bowls, spoons, masks, rattles, and canoes. Cedar bark provided material for mats and clothing.

Northwest Coast art has one of the most distinctive styles in Native American art. Basically an expression of the peoples' relationship to mythological animals, their art portrayed these creatures in symbolic, stylized forms, which often show spiritual messages being transferred from creature to human. Particular features identified certain animals: big front teeth and a large, usually crosshatched, tail represented a beaver; the bear had a protruding tongue. At the joints of the body, Northwest Coast artists often placed an eyelike element.

The Tsimshian and Tlingit were known for their Chilkat blankets made of woven goat hair and cedar bark. These finely woven, fringed blankets also depicted various animals in the Northwest Coast style. They still make some of these blankets today.

*The central design of this Chilkat blanket features a human face symbolizing the body of a bird. Such fine blankets are still woven by Tlingit women.*

All the Northwest Coast tribes also made fine twined baskets. The Salishan tribes used the imbricated coiled technique. The Nootka and other tribes still produce high quality basketry.

Today, groups such as the Kwakiutl carve totem poles and other finely crafted articles. The Indian Arts and Crafts Board encourages woodcarvers to keep alive their traditional arts.

kets for lower ranking guests to canoes or marmot pelt robes for higher ranking individuals. Each guest had to be fed and housed for as long as twelve days, a major task in itself. For the ceremonial part of the potlatch, the host's lineage also had to make masks and equipment and practice dances and songs in order to give perfect performances. Finally, the host had to prepare spiritually for the event for a year in advance.

There was a dark side to Northwest Coast life: the tribes practiced warfare to expand their lands, and forced captured prisoners into slavery. In wars against the poorer and weaker tribes living farther south along the California coast and in the interior of their own region, Northwest Coast peoples captured men, women, and children to be slaves. Only high ranking men and women were permitted to own slaves, who were considered to be extremely valuable property. Not only did slaves relieve their owners of menial and back-

breaking tasks, but they were also visible evidence of their owners' wealth and status. Slaves slept in their owners' households and performed a range of tasks from food preparation to chopping down trees.

Slaves had little hope of ever gaining their freedom, and they lived in constant fear that their owners would sacrifice them at the next potlatch. When a wealthy family completed a new dwelling, tradition dictated that the slaves be killed and thrown into the holes before the great carved doorway posts could be placed. Once in a while, a slave might be freed; at the traditional feast honoring children whose ears were to be pierced for earrings, a slave had to be freed for each child who was honored.

Slaves could also be ransomed. When Tlingits were taken into slavery as war captives, their people ransomed them as soon as possible because they believed such captivity was a disgrace to the entire clan. A Tlingit clan never forgot this humiliation.

## EUROPEAN CONTACT

The earliest record of European contact with the Northwest Coast peoples dates to 1741, when a Russian explorer sailed his ship into the harbor of what is now Sitka, Alaska. The Northwest Coast peoples, who often traded with other Indians, were eager to trade with the Europeans for new materials. They began trading sea otter pelts and other furs for iron implements and firearms. Some tribes often used these guns to kill their tribal neighbors.

In the trading period before settlement, white-Indian relations were remarkably peaceful. European traders wanted Indians to maintain their culture so that the native peoples could continue supplying the valuable sea otter pelts. The Indians did not feel threatened because contact with whites tended to be brief and involved only a few people at a time. These limited conditions of contact led to peaceful relations between the two groups.

As in every case of white-Indian contact, however, the most destructive aspect was disease. In the first century of contact, Europeans introduced smallpox, malaria, measles, influenza, dysentery, whooping cough, typhoid fever, and typhus. The Bella Coola lost almost half their population in the smallpox epidemic of 1836–1837.

Eventually, white settlers moved into the Northwest Coast, wanting Indian land. In order to prevent the United States from claiming Vancouver Island, the British government began to encourage settlement there in 1849. In the 1850s, treaties were made with the tribes of British Columbia to take over Indian lands. After Alaska became United States territory in 1867, the Indians of southeast Alaska were also under pressure to give up their lands to non-natives.

With the settlers arrived Christian missionaries. The missionaries did help the Northwest Coast

*Members of the Kwakiutl Shaman's Society surround the Kwakiutl Hamatsa, who represents the Cannibal Spirit. The society includes malevolent bird-spirits such as the Crooked Beak of Heaven; Raven; and the Hoxhox; as well as less terrifying spirits such as the woman, who symbolizes the weather, and the horned mountain goat, who represents mountain climbers.*

peoples to learn English and other skills that enabled them to survive in white society. But they also waged an active war against traditional Indian practices. Missionaries and government officials opposed the potlatch because it seemed wasteful to them and because it affirmed native culture. The potlatch was the living expression of Northwest Coast spirituality, political systems, and hereditary rights.

The institution of the potlatch changed dramatically in the nineteenth century. In the early days, even wealthy chiefs gave only a few potlatches in a lifetime because each required such a major outlay of resources. The potlatch was a rare and serious occasion because it commemorated the shared history and traditions of the group; it cemented the group's loyalty and sense of belonging.

The Europeans brought unimagined wealth to the peoples of the Northwest Coast in the form of mass-produced European goods, such as Hudson Bay Company blankets. This influx of trade goods distorted the value of goods traditionally given in the potlatch. Handmade cedar bark blankets seemed less valuable in comparison with the cheaply produced European blankets. With access to so much material wealth, potlatches became both increasingly common and more elaborate.

Because Europeans wanted a peaceful setting for their trading networks, they discouraged the Indians from going to war among themselves by favoring native leaders who could keep peace. They rewarded such leaders with trade benefits. Without warfare, long an accepted outlet for aggression, the people became fiercely competitive in the potlatch, vying to see who could give the most and shame their rival. The original cultural meaning of the potlatch was lost.

The final blow came in 1884, when Christian missionaries persuaded the Canadian government to outlaw the potlatch. It was not until 1951 that the government changed this law. The potlatch, so deeply rooted in the culture and traditions of the Northwest Coast, was finally restored.

## CHIEF SEATTLE

Seattle (1786–1866) was a famous Suquamish chief. In 1792, he saw the British explorer George Vancouver sail into Puget Sound in his ship, the *Discovery*. Seattle was impressed by the friendliness of Vancouver and his men and decided that peace, not war, was the right path.

This decision marked a major change in his life. As a young man, he had led an alliance of six tribes against the "horse tribes" to the northeast. This successful undertaking had won him the title of Chief of the Allied Tribes (the Duwamish Confederacy). After contact with Vancouver and his men, however, he decided to devote the rest of his life to promoting peace.

Chief Seattle is buried just outside the present-day city of Seattle. His grave is marked with a granite shaft inscribed, "Seattle, Chief of the Suquamish and Allied tribes, died June 7, 1866, the firm friend of the Whites, and for him the City of Seattle was named by its founders." Boy Scouts conduct a memorial ceremony there each year.

# CHAPTER SIX

# CALIFORNIA

*The White people never cared for land or deer or bear. When we Indians kill meat, we eat it all up. When we dig roots we make little holes....When we burn grass for grasshoppers, we don't ruin things. We shake down acorns and pinenuts. We don't chop down the trees. We only use dead wood. But the White people plow up the ground, pull down the trees, kill everything. The tree says, "Don't. I am sore. Don't hurt me." But they chop it down and cut it up. The spirit of the land hates them. They blast out trees and stir it up to its depths. They saw up trees. That hurts them....How can the spirit of the earth like the White man?...Everywhere the White man has touched it, it is sore.*

—A holy Wintu woman, 1950s

# LANGUAGES OF THE TRIBES OF CALIFORNIA

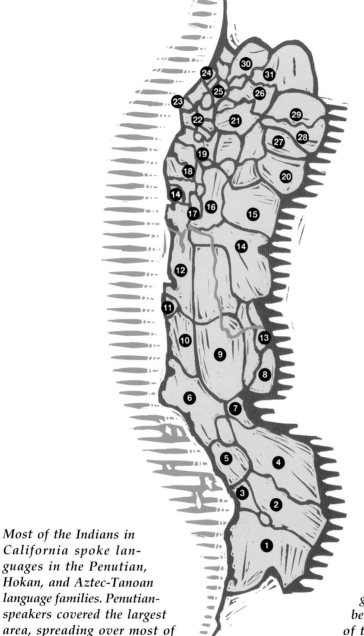

| 1. Digueño | 17. Wappo |
| 2. Cahuilla | 18. Pomo |
| 3. Luiseño | 19. Yuki |
| 4. Serrano | 20. Maidu |
| 5. Gabrieliño | 21. Wintu |
| 6. Chumash | 22. Athabascan |
| 7. Kwaiisu | 23. Wiyot |
| 8. Tubatulabal | 24. Yurok |
| 9. Yokuts | 25. Karuk and |
| 10. Salinan | Chimariko |
| 11. Esselen | 26. Shasta |
| 12. Costanoan | 27. Atsugewi |
| 13. Mono | 28. Achomawi |
| 14. Miwok | 29. Modoc |
| 15. Nisenan | 30. Takelma |
| 16. Patwin | 31. Klamath |

*Most of the Indians in California spoke languages in the Penutian, Hokan, and Aztec-Tanoan language families. Penutian-speakers covered the largest area, spreading over most of central California; this included tribes such as the Miwok, Costanoan, Yokuts, Maidu, Wintu, Klamath, and Modoc. Hokan-speakers lived in small pockets from today's Oregon to Mexico; Yana, Karuk, Shasta, Yuki, and Pomo peoples spoke Hokan languages, which is probably the oldest California language group. Aztec-Tanoan-speakers (all who were in the Shoshonean subfamily) included the Kern River, Mission, and Mono tribes. Tribes in north-central and northern California spoke Athabascan and Algonquian.*

*Each language family includes languages that are very different. For example, two languages in the Penutian language family could be as different as English is from German. Each of the sixty-four to eighty different California languages could be divided even further into dialects of the same language. Sadly, only a little more than twenty-four of these languages have survived through the middle of the twentieth century. Some of these are so-called "terminal" languages, spoken by only a few elderly people. When these people die, no native speakers of these languages will exist. Imagine the sense of silent isolation that you would feel if everyone around you were speaking a foreign language and you were the only person left who spoke English.*

California was blessed with a pleasant climate and all the rain that the Sierras withheld from the Great Basin. For California's native peoples, a wide range of animals and plants provided food and plants, and trees for making shelter, clothing, and tools were everywhere.

When the white man arrived in California in the eighteenth century, there were as many as 133,500 Indians living there. They spoke between sixty-four and eighty different languages, giving California the greatest diversity of Indian languages in any North American culture area.

Despite differences in languages, the Indians of California shared a similar lifestyle, living in villages made up of families that were related through the men. Sometimes several villages formed a tribelet—a loose, unstructured association. The pleasant California climate and diverse geography meant that there were abundant rivers and streams and plentiful resources for making food, housing, and

clothing. The people had little need of elaborate clothing or housing and lived in fairly temporary dwellings. Clothing was not always necessary in the relatively mild California climate, so in warm weather, men often wore nothing at all, while women generally wore a knee-length shredded fiber apron that covered them in front and back. For protection from the winter cold, men and women wore rabbit skin robes much like those of the Great Basin Indians. Acorns were their staple food, supplemented with other wild plants, game, and fish. Basket making was the California Indians' main form of artistic expression.

Some of the northern California groups were as skilled in woodworking as the peoples of the Northwest Coast, and they made dugout canoes and sturdy plank houses similar to those of their neighbors to the north; salmon was also central to their diet. California tribes that bordered the Southwest, such as the Yumans (who are covered in

*Top: Scarlet scalps from pileated woodpeckers on bands of white fur decorate the headbands of these Hupa Jumping Dancers, whose dances renewed the world for the coming year. Left: Women carefully prepare acorn meal, an important food for California Indians.*

the next chapter), farmed and focused on warfare like their Southwestern neighbors.

The Pomos, most of whom lived north of San Francisco in what are now Sonoma, Lake, and Mendocino counties, were among the most fortunate California Indians because they lived in an area with a moderate year-round climate and a great abundance of plants and game. Some eight thousand Pomos lived in fifty self-sufficient communities. They were close to the rugged coastline with its abundance of marine resources, the Russian River country with its grassy rolling hills and oak trees, and Clear Lake with its fish, waterfowl, game, and proliferation of wild plants.

*Alosa Williams, a Shasta woman, in her finery. Shasta women wove finely twined basketry hats in which the wefts of conifer roots were covered with strands of glossy yellow bear grass and shiny black fern stem. The Shasta used the full-twist overlay strand technique so that the design showed on the inside and the outside of the hat.*

fowl, which were a major source of food from November until mid-February. Although hunting was usually a communal project, a man sometimes went out alone to catch an occasional deer, rabbit, quail, or waterfowl. During communal hunts, a good marksman was chosen to wear a deer-head mask and shoot the deer while the other hunters drove the animals toward him. Sometimes they built a corral into which they herded the animals. If they were to be successful, all men had to prepare themselves spiritually before the hunt.

In the long, quiet days before the white man intruded into their homeland, California's natural abundance made food gathering easy. By simply responding to the rhythms of the bountiful land around them, the Indians found all the food they needed. The fall acorn harvest in October and November was a major event in their lives. Men and boys climbed the great oak trees to shake the nuts loose, while women and girls collected the fallen bounty. Acorns take a great deal of preparation before they can be eaten because they contain tannin, a bitter-tasting substance that causes indigestion. After drying, hulling, and pulverizing the acorns into flour, women would leach them in hot water to remove the tannin. They then boiled the meal in a tight-meshed basket to make acorn mush. Sometimes, they molded the acorn meal into cakes, which they baked in the fire's hot ashes.

While the women were busy with their acorn gathering and preparation, the men caught water-

At the end of February, the men, using conical basketry traps, were able to catch suckers, the first fish to go up the creeks to spawn. In mid-March the pikes swam upstream; the Indians speared these with a fish gig. As the water became warmer, the hitch and chay swam up; the Pomo caught these in long basketry traps in a fish dam made of brush. In April, the Eastern Pomo left their main village for fish camps along the edge of Clear Lake, where they used fish traps and nets to catch blackfish and native carp. They dried, stored, and ate these fish throughout the rest of the year. The Eastern Pomo were able to catch such a surplus of fish that they traded them for beads to the Northern and Central Pomo.

As the men fished, the women gathered clover. In June they collected clams and tule (bulrushes) from the marshes that almost completely surrounded the lake. The Eastern and Southeastern Pomo used tule for houses, boats, and clothing. They also made women's skirts and men's mantles, moccasins, and leggings out of tule. They served their food on tule mats and used shredded tule for bedding and babies' diapers. They ate the tender shoots and roots of the tule as well.

Later in June, the Pomo moved camp to the hills, where the women dug up roots. In July, they returned to the main village with their roots, tule, and clams. August and September found them gathering pinole seed and traveling to the coast to collect salt and other marine resources.

The ease and certainty of their food supply allowed the Pomo to build fairly substantial houses in permanent locations. Only in the summer and autumn, when they were gathering wild plants and hunting game animals, did the Pomo live in temporary brush shelters. During the rest of the year, the coastal Pomo lived in single-family tipi-like dwellings, about 10 to 15 feet (3 to 4.5m) in diameter, covered with redwood bark or wood. The Russian River Pomo had multifamily oval, dome-

## WINTU SONGS OF SPIRITS

### LIGHTNING
I bear the sucker-torch to the western tree ridge.
Behold me! first born and greatest.

### OLELBIS (THE CREATOR)
I am great above.
I tan the black cloud.

### HAU (RED FOX)
On the stone ridge east I go.
On the white road I, Hau, crouching go.
I, Hau, whistle on the road of stars.

### POLAR STAR
The circuit of the earth which you see,
The scattering of stars in the sky which you see,
All that is the place for my hair.

*A Pomo man from Clear Lake sits in his boat constructed from bundles of tule rushes. Such unsinkable reed rafts were ideal for crossing rivers and streams.*

## THE LUISEÑO ORIGIN MYTH

*In the beginning there was only empty space. The earth and the sky did not exist. Two clouds came into this space who were brother and sister. The clouds kept changing into different forms until the brother became Sky and the sister became Earth. Their union produced animals who were people. The first people migrated from place to place until they reached their homelands. When the all-powerful god, Wiyó-t, who rules the people, died and was cremated, his body lived in the moon. His death brought death to the world. By dying, Wiyó-t determined the nature of the mourning ceremony [of the Luiseño]. Later, another god, Chingichngish, was born to instruct the people in ceremonial rites.*

shaped houses 25 to 30 feet (7.6 to 9.1m) in length in their permanent villages. To build these houses, they first stuck slender poles into the ground in an oval formation. Then they bent the poles over, tying them at the top. To add strength to the structure, they added more poles. Overlapping layers of coarse grass covered the wooden framework. The Clear Lake Pomo thatched their houses with tule instead of grass, but otherwise their homes resembled those of the Russian River Pomo.

Pomo men took daily sweat baths in the sweat lodge, a 15- to 20-foot (4.5 to 6m) brush and earth structure with a 4-foot (1.2m) -deep central fire pit. The fire provided intense heat, making the men sweat and thus purify themselves.

At the center of the village was the dance house, or "singing lodge," a partially underground,

*These Monache Indians (often called the Western Mono) lived on the western slope of the Sierra Nevada in conical houses covered with slabs of cedar bark. Their descendants live on the Tule River Reservation, near Porterville.*

earth-covered building some 40 to 60 feet (12.1 to 18.2m) across. At the heart of each building in the village—family homes, sweat lodges, and singing lodge—was the glowing fire made sacred by its life-giving quality.

The abundance of resources available to the Indians of California meant that they did not have to develop elaborate techniques for gathering and hunting. Instead, they were able to channel their creativity into basketry. The California Indians made some of the finest baskets of all Native Americans; the Pomo wove some of the most beautiful baskets in the world.

The Pomo used several techniques, including coiling and twining, and thirty or more different plant materials for their baskets. Some Pomo baskets reached 3 feet (0.9m) in diameter, while others were as small as a thimble. Even Pomo men wove, producing carrying baskets, cradles, fishtraps, and mats, although it was Pomo women who did most of the weaving. For everyday use they made cooking baskets, burden and storage baskets, sifters, and trays for winnowing.

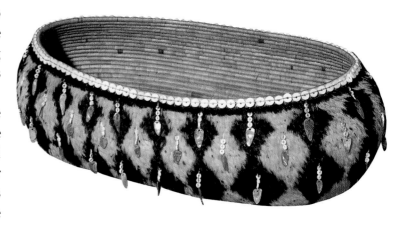

*This coiled basket is decorated with yellow and black feathers, and shell and abalone ornaments.*

They also wove fine gift baskets that were usually black and red in a wide variety of designs. Most Pomo women knew fifteen to twenty distinct patterns. So sophisticated were the Pomo as basket makers that they even named design elements and patterns. For further decoration, they often added clamshell disks as well as brilliantly colored feathers to the baskets. Sadly, today, the art of basketry is almost extinct.

*A Miwok conical house. These structures were built at lower elevations in Central Sierra Miwok territory by tying tule mats to a framework of poles.*

# ARTS AND CRAFTS

*Mary Benson, a famous Pomo basket weaver, at the turn of the century. Traditionally, Pomo weavers wove willow, sedge root, bullrush root, and redbud bark, often inserting small feathers in the stitches to give the outside of the basket a soft, velvety appearance.*

California tribes are often divided into three geographical areas, from north to south. The small groups, known as Mission Indians, who lived in southern California, once made finely woven coiled baskets in rich red-brown tones, with rattlesnake designs. Their pottery was an unpainted red ware. They also carved naturalistic soapstone animals inset with shell beads.

The central California groups specialized in basketry. They produced little woodwork and no pottery. The designs and forms of their baskets emphasized the technical excellence of their weaving. Using coiled and twined techniques, as well as some wickerwork, the women made baskets decorated with brightly colored feathers and shell pendants. Pomo baskets were of particularly fine quality. They made baskets as large as 3 feet (0.9m) in diameter and as small as half an inch (1.2cm).

The peoples of northern California were influenced by the Northwest Coast culture: like their northern woodworking neighbors, they made plank houses and dugout canoes. Northern California Indians were also known for crafting elk antler spoons with delicately carved handles. Their baskets equaled those of the central Californians in technique. Karok and Yurok basket makers created some of the finest examples, which were often decorated with yellow porcupine quills and the rich brown maidenhair fern stems.

Although some women were still weaving fine baskets at the turn of the century, the art of basketry is nearly lost today.

*Nievas Chavaz and her baby, Luiseño Indians on the Pala Reservation around the turn of the century. Known as one of the "Mission Tribes," the Luiseño was one of the largest tribes in southern California at the time of Spanish contact.*

The birth of a child was a time of joyous celebration and gift-giving between the father's and the mother's families. While the mother was pregnant, the father's family gave her a special kind of beautiful necklace. When the child was born, the mother's family gave her a valuable bead belt and the most precious of baskets, woven with the red topknots of woodpeckers. The families exchanged more ritual gifts following the birth of the child.

While his wife was giving birth, the husband observed the couvade—he had to stay confined indoors, and could not hunt, travel, or gamble for a month. The couvade, practiced by many California Indians, is a custom shared by many cultures around the world. It is the male equivalent of the female birth experience and is believed to ensure the health of the child and the mother.

When a Pomo girl had her first menstrual period, she was isolated in a small tule structure attached to her house. She purified herself during this time by lying on a bed made of tule placed over a bed of coals, so that she was bathed in steam. Her only food was acorn mush and pinole. Her aunt or mother fed her, combed her hair, and scratched her if necessary; she was not allowed to touch her own body. On the fourth night or fifth morning, she bathed, then put on a skirt, beads, and a hairnet. She then ground a basketful of acorns into meal. She leached them and cooked them, feeding this acorn mush to her family and friends. The basket she used was saved and would be used again only for the first menstruation of her sisters.

At about eight years old, a boy was given a hairnet and a toy bow and arrows; then he was bathed in angelica root water at a feast. There was no specific ceremony for boys reaching puberty.

Young people, with the approval of their families, made their own decisions as to whom they would marry. The first formal commitment to marriage came when the future son-in-law spent the night at his bride's house. Her parents had to be willing to call him "son-in-law" or else he could not stay. The next morning, the families of the bride and groom exchanged presents—food, beads, rabbit skin blankets, and fine baskets. Instead of the newly married couple receiving the gifts, however, their families were the recipients.

The Pomo cremated their dead until about 1880, when white pressure made them stop this custom. They began mourning before a person died, expressing their heartfelt grief in many ways. Both men and women cried, and women scratched their faces. The body was left in the house for three or four days as people came in to bring gifts, including robes, blankets, beads, and fine baskets. The relatives would later present the givers with gifts of equal value. The body was cremated on a funeral pyre, face down, with the head pointed south. The women sang mourning songs. To show their state of mourning, both men and women cut their normally long hair. Mourning for important people and the young lasted a year.

Pomo shamans specialized either in curing or in ceremonies. The curing shamans ensured the health of individuals and of the entire community.

## ISHI

Ishi (1857–1914) was the last Yahi Indian. In August 1911, after the rest of his tribe had died out, he left his home in the foothills of Mount Lassen to walk to Oroville. There, the authorities could not decide what to do with him. Alfred Kroeber and T.T. Waterman of the University of California at Berkeley took him in. They provided him a room in the museum at the university and tried to learn all that they could about his culture. They gave him the name Ishi, Yahi for "man." Ishi learned some English and adapted well to his new life. For the next three years, he enjoyed the wonders of San Francisco, until he died of tuberculosis. Alfred Kroeber described him as "the most patient man I ever knew...He had mastered the philosophy of patience, without trace either of self-pity or bitterness to dull the purity of his cheerful enduringness."

*With Ishi's death, the collective experience of his tribe was irretrievably lost.*

A Karuk man wears dance clothing. In their annual celebrations, Karuks performed rituals meant to both renew the earth and protect its seasonal cycles.

## THE KARUK TRIBE

The Karuk (Karok) Tribe of northern California is renewing its culture and religion. The Karuk homeland is the area around the Klamath River Canyon between Seiad Valley in the north and Bluff Creek in the south. The Yurok, Hupa, Tolowa, and Shasta tribes all lived nearby. The Karuk were fortunate to remain isolated until the 1820s, when white trappers invaded the region. After an influx of white settlers following the gold rush, the Karuk had to fight to keep their traditions and their land.

In 1985, there were three thousand Karuks living in more than 215 miles (344km) of rugged terrain. Today, most of the people live in the towns of Eureka, Orleans, Happy Camp, and Yreka.

Many people have gained a sense of tribal renewal from taking classes on Karuk language and culture that were started in the 1970s. The tribe completed a dictionary of their language. The Karuk have also begun performing their traditional dances. Each year they now celebrate *Pikiavish,* which means World Renewal Ceremony; they have brought back this important celebration, which had last been performed in 1912.

The Pomo believed that most forms of illness were caused by poisoning. In order to avoid poisoning, the people followed strict rules of etiquette. Ghosts could also cause illness.

The Kuksu cult was a society that focused on performing rites to ensure group well-being. Some Kuksu rituals centered on fertility and the harvesting of the first fruit, while others emphasized protection against dangerous aspects of nature.

The Pomo held the Kuksu ceremony, which included dances in the earth-covered house, every year in a different village. Boys were initiated between the ages of ten and twelve in their ritual and professional roles. Members of the Kuksu society, impersonating the Kuksu or other sacred beings, instructed the boys in sacred knowledge.

Other public Pomo ceremonies focused specifically on food and crops. There were first-fruits cere-monies for acorns, manzanita, wild strawberries, and other important foods. Women carried or wore flowers in the Lole dance.

The Hupa, Yurok, and Karuk peoples of northern California held World Renewal ceremonies every year. Although these rituals to "firm up the earth" and ensure good fortune were held at different times of year, depending upon the group, they shared a similar purpose and form. In the first part, which was highly sacred, a specially designated man traveled to a number of sacred locations where he carried out rites to ensure nature's renewal. The second, more social, part included the Jumping Dance—dancers performed crouching, leaping movements—and the White Deerskin Dance, in which participants carried poles around which they had draped entire deerskins, with the rarer white deerskins being more desirable.

*By 1910, the term "Mission Indians" referred to all Indians whose ancestors had been forced into the Spanish missions between San Francisco and San Diego, like those pictured in this engraving, who are receiving instruction at a mission. Today, many Indians hate this term and insist upon the use of their tribal or band designation.*

# EUROPEAN CONTACT

In 1542, the Chumash Indians of California, the first to encounter Europeans, met some Spanish missionaries. For many years, Spain's major interest in California had been in locating a suitable harbor for galleons sailing between Mexico and the Philippines. Only when Britain and Russia appeared to challenge Spain's claim to California did the Spanish send missionaries to strengthen their control of the area.

In 1769, the first mission was established in California. The Spanish felt that the conversion of the Indians to Roman Catholicism would stop the influence of British Protestantism and Russian Orthodoxy. The Spanish also perceived the Indians as a vast labor force for the development of New Spain.

Over the course of the next sixty-five years, the missionaries totally destroyed almost every aspect of California Indian culture. The Indians were forced to wear clothes, to cultivate mission farms, to tend mission herds, to adopt Christianity, to speak Spanish, and to live in mission towns. With whites and Indians living in such close quarters, diseases to which the people had no immunity quickly destroyed much of the native population.

The Mission Period ended in 1821 with Mexico's independence from Spain, but the mission Indians no longer had a culture to which they could return. They had worked the mission fields as peasants and obeyed the missionaries' rules too well: they had become entirely dependent upon the priests for their food and shelter.

In 1846, the United States acquired California, leading to an influx of white settlers. Many Indian groups, such as the Luiseño and Chumash, were already near extinction. The Pomo, who lived north of the Spanish missions, had survived Catholicism, but the California gold rush of 1848 wiped out their culture when miners and then settlers swarmed into their territory.

## THE YANA

The Yana people, who included the Northern and Southern Yana and Yahi, lived in the upper Sacramento River valley and foothills east of the river. They were outnumbered by their Wintu neighbors, who pushed the Yana farther into the hills. White settlers came into the area in 1847. By 1848, the California-Oregon trail crossed their territory. When it became increasingly difficult for the Yana to obtain food, they began raiding white cabins. Within twenty years, the Yana population declined from 1,900 to fewer than a hundred.

The Hupa were the most fortunate of California Indians because they lived in an inaccessible valley that protected them until 1864, when Congress established a reservation in their homeland. Although their traditional lifestyle has changed, the Hupa have been able to remain self-sufficient and to adjust to change at a reasonable pace. Today they are farmers, ranchers, and construction workers.

*Girls learn to sew at the Sherman Institute in Riverside, California, a nonreservation boarding school where Indians were taught to abandon their own culture in favor of white culture.*

# CHAPTER SEVEN

# >THE<
# SOUTHWEST

*We say Nahasdzáán Shimà:*
*Earth, My Mother.*
*We are made from her.*
*Even though she takes us daily,*
*We will become part of*
*    her again.*
*For we ARE her.*

*The Earth is Our Mother.*
*The Sky is Our Father.*
*Just as a man gives his wife*
*    beautiful things to wear,*
*So Our Father Sky does the same.*
*He sends rain down on Mother*
*    Earth,*
*And because of the rain the*
*    plants grow,*
*And flowers appear of many*
*    different colors.*
*She in turn provides food for him.*
*He dresses her as a man would*
*    dress his woman.*
*He moves clouds and male rain.*

*He moves dark mists and*
*    female rain.*
*Dark mists cloak the ground,*
*And plants grow with many*
*    colored blossoms.*
*The plants with colored blossoms*
*    are her dress.*
*It wears out. Yes, the earth's cover*
*    wears out.*
*The plants ripen and fade away*
*    in the fall.*
*Then in the spring when the rains*
*    come again*
*Mother Earth once again puts on*
*    her finery.*
*The plants are restored again in*
*    beauty.*
*This is what the stories of the*
*    Elders say.*

*—*George Blueeyes,
Navajo, in *Between Sacred*
*Mountains,* 1982

# LANGUAGES OF THE TRIBES OF THE SOUTHWEST

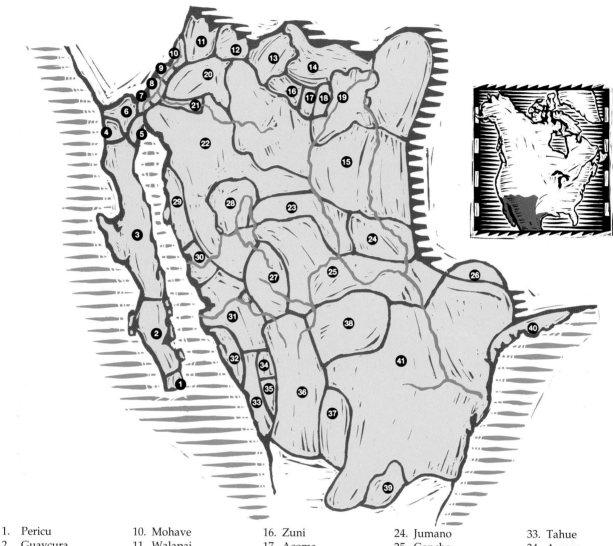

| | | | | |
|---|---|---|---|---|
| 1. Pericu | 10. Mohave | 16. Zuni | 24. Jumano | 33. Tahue |
| 2. Guaycura | 11. Walapai | 17. Acoma | 25. Concho | 34. Acaxee |
| 3. Cochimi | 12. Havasupai | 18. Laguna | 26. Cacaxtes | 35. Xixime |
| 4. Nakipa | 13. Hopi | 19. Rio Grande Pueblos | 27. Tarahumara | 36. Tepehuan |
| 5. Kiliwa | 14. Navajo | 20. Yavapai | 28. Opata | 37. Zacatec |
| 6. Paipai | 15. Western, | 21. Maricopa | 29. Seri | 38. Toboso |
| 7. Cocopa |     Chiricahua, | 22. Tohono O'odham | 30. Yaqui | 39. Pame |
| 8. Quechan (Yuma) |     Jicarilla, and |     and Pima | 31. Mayo | 40. Karankawa |
| 9. Halchidoma |     Mescalero Apache | 23. Suma | 32. Guasave | 41. Insufficient data |

The Hokan-Coahuiltecan linguistic stock includes the Upland Yumans—the Havasupai, Walapai, and Yavapai of northern Arizona—and the River Yumans —the Cocopa, Maricopa, Mohave, and Yuma—who originally lived on the border between southern California and Arizona. The Hopi, Piman, Yaqui, and Tanoan pueblos speak languages in the Aztec-Tanoan linguistic stock, related to those spoken by the Utes of the Great Basin and the Aztecs of Mexico. The Navajo and various Apache groups speak Athabascan (in the Nadene linguistic stock), which connects them to many of the peoples in the Northwest Coast region.

Some linguists classify Zuni in the Penutian linguistic stock while others feel that Zuni is a language isolate. The people of the pueblos of Acoma, Laguna, and the Rio Grande area (the pueblos of San Felipe, Santa Ana, Zia, Santo Domingo, and Cochiti) speak the Keresan language.

The American Southwest is a magnificent land of great variety: the plunging blue-green waterfall of Havasu Canyon; the saguaro cactus forests of the Sonoran Desert (home to the Ranchería tribes); the broad, cloud-dappled valley of the Little Colorado River; the mountain grasslands of the Kaibab Plateau (home of the Navajo); the fragrant high pine forests of the Sacramento Mountains (of the Apache); the orange sandstone cliffs of the Hopi mesas; and the snow-encrusted mountains surrounding Taos Blue Lake (home to the Puebloan peoples). This dramatic landscape is home to three distinct native cultures. Farming and hunting supported the Ranchería tribes: the Yumans (Yuma, Mohave, Halchidoma, Kohuana, Kavelchadom, Havasupai, Walapai, and Yavapai); Pimans (Pima and Tohono O'odham); and Yaqui.

The largest tribe in North America, the Navajo (and their linguistic cousins, the Apache), arrived in the Southwest as nomadic hunters but the Navajo later became farmers and pastoralists. The Puebloan peoples lived (and still live) in settled villages in northern New Mexico and Arizona.

The Southwest includes the present-day states of Arizona and New Mexico with extensions into southern Utah and southwestern Colorado. It is here that we find the oldest continuous record of human habitation in North America outside of Mexico. Archaeologists continue to uncover pithouses, potsherds, petroglyphs, and worked stone implements that were made hundreds of years ago. Scientists estimate that the Hopi pueblo at Oraibi in northern Arizona has been there for nearly a thousand years.

*Top: Women from Acoma Pueblo fill their pottery jars from a cistern.*
*Left: Kupishtaya, chief of the lightning makers, in a kiva mural from Kuaua, a New Mexico pueblo. Established in the fourteenth century, Kuaua was a meeting ground for two prehistoric cultures, the Anasazi and the Mogollon.*

# THE RANCHERÍA TRIBES

In the early 1600s, the Spaniards called most of the Indians they encountered in the Southwest ranchería (Spanish for "camp") people because within each settlement the houses were often set far apart from each other, sometimes with as much as half a mile (0.8km) between them. The ranchería people were farmers, but most of them shifted from one location to another during the year, supplementing their diet by hunting and gathering. As discussed in this chapter, there are important cultural differences among the peoples—the Yumans, the Pimans, and the Yaqui—who followed this way of life.

## THE RIVER YUMANS

At the delta of the lower part of the Colorado River lies a narrow swatch of fertile land. This area floods each spring when the snow melts in the Rocky Mountains, bringing fertile soil that made farming without irrigation possible for the River Yumans who lived there. Even in the sun's intense summer heat, the roots of the plants received plenty of moisture from the riverbank soil.

A number of tribes, including the Mohave, Yuma, Halchidoma, Kohuana, and Kavelchadom, lived in sprawling villages that stretched out across this fertile valley for several miles. Five miles (8km) or so separated one settlement from the next.

During most of the year the people slept under flat-topped, open-sided ramadas. (A ramada is a structure made of upright posts that support roof beams that are covered with boughs.) They wintered in low, rectangular, earth-covered houses that blended in well with the surrounding landscape. By the time that they had moved into their winter quarters, they had brought in their autumn harvest of corn, beans, pumpkins, and melons. The other half of their food came from hunting and gathering. The men caught rabbits and fished for squaw fish, mullet, bony tail, and hump-backed suckers; the women gathered mesquite beans, screw beans, and piñon nuts.

The Mohave were fierce fighters who battled other tribes to gain prestige. They fought formal hand-to-hand battles, with the warriors arranged in lines facing each other. A single war chief led warriors divided into three ranks: archers (with longbows and untipped arrows of sharpened arrowweed); clubbers (who used hardwood clubs to inflict most of the damage in hand-to-hand fighting); and stickmen (who finished off the enemy wounded). They continued to fight until all the warriors on one side had been killed or soundly defeated.

*Living in a desert climate, the Mohave needed little clothing. These Mohave decorated their bodies with painted designs typical of the 1850s. The men wear long breechclouts, the woman a double skirt of bark fiber. Some Mohave also wore tattoos, as seen on the woman's chin.*

During the late 1700s and the early 1800s, the Mohave from the north joined the Yuma from the south to attack the Halchidoma, Kohuana, and Kavelchadom Indians, who lived in between the Mohave and the Yuma. The remaining members of these three tribes merged with the Maricopa and moved eastward along the Gila River, where they became allies of the Pima. In 1857, the Yuma and Mohave warriors came eastward again to attack the Maricopa forces. This time, however, the Pima helped the besieged tribes to thoroughly defeat the war-hungry Mohave and Yuma.

## THE UPLAND YUMANS

The water of Havasu Falls plunges into a dazzling blue-green pool that gives its name to the Havasupai, "The People of the Blue-Green Water." For over nine hundred years, from early spring until mid-October, they have lived in Cataract Canyon, a high-walled canyon threaded by the life-giving Colorado River. The eroded vertical walls of this side branch of the Grand Canyon reach upward to the adjoining plateau.

The Colorado River makes it possible for the Havasupai to farm; they grow corn, beans, squash, melons, tobacco, and sunflowers. The Havasupai have never taken their surroundings for granted.

Even today, many of them believe that the Colorado flooded in 1993 because people in Arizona were abusing the water, wasting it, and not giving thanks for it.

The Havasupai learned how to farm from their Hopi neighbors, from whom they also borrowed rituals such as prayers for corn planting, prayer sticks, a rain dance, and masked dancing.

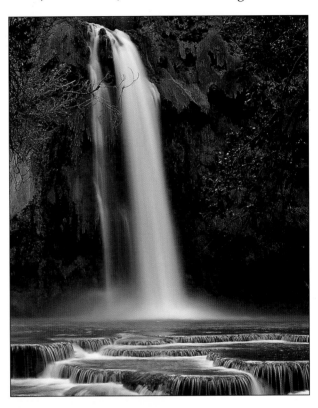

*Above: The Havasu Falls, from which the Havasupai took their name—"The People of the Blue-Green Water." Left: A Havasu tent-shaped shelter with a ridge pole. The Havasupai also built domed, conical, and rectangular houses.*

*A Havasupai rests before entering his sweat lodge, an important place for spiritual and physical purification.*

Sweat lodges played an important role in traditional Havasupai culture. In addition to ceremonial sweats, which they used for purification, they also took part in social sweats. When they finished their work, they relaxed in the sweat lodge, catching up on the local news and exchanging gossip. They even played games (such as gambling games) inside the sweat lodge. Afterward, they felt clean and pure because they had sweat out all their worries.

The Havasupai were luckier than the other Upland Yuman groups, the Walapai and the Yavapai, who had to depend on hunting and gathering to make a living. These tribes were forced to move constantly to survive, while the Havasupai were able to spend half the year in Cataract Canyon, tending their fields.

The Walapai, whose name means "Pine Tree People," lived south of the Grand Canyon in an arid land basically unsuitable for farming. In spring and summer they left their village so that the women could gather seeds, berries, roots, and fruits, while the men hunted deer, rabbit, antelope, and mountain sheep. They covered their dome-shaped homes with juniper bark or thatch over a wooden framework.

The Yavapai, "The People of the Sun" or "The Crooked Mouth People," shared a culture similar to that of the Walapai and the Havasupai although they ranged over a much greater area—approximately 20,000 square miles (51,800 sq km). The Southeastern, Northeastern, and Western tribal divisions of the Yavapai divided even further into localized bands that ranged over much of Arizona. The Apache strongly influenced the Southeastern Yavapai, who adopted some Apache practices, including sharing clan membership through women; a mother-in-law taboo (a man was supposed to avoid prolonged contact with his wife's mother); tule pollen ceremonies; and masked dancers.

# THE PIMANS

The Tohono O'odham were, and still are, people of the desert. Their homeland is dry, the parched earth always sadly in need of rain; even early in the morning on a spring day, the heat blisters exposed skin. The Tohono O'odham have been masters of survival, for they have lived in a rugged environment where poor judgment could mean certain death. A person trying to survive in Tohono O'odham territory without the tribal knowledge would probably die within days from lack of water and the sun's burning heat.

Early explorers named these people Papago—"bean eater"—because tepary and mesquite beans were such an important part of their diet. They have always called themselves Tohono O'odham, which means "Desert People" in their language; in the 1980s, the tribal council voted to adopt this name.

Baboquivari, a distinctive purple peak visible on the western horizon from Tucson, is their sacred mountain, home of the spirit of Elder Brother, I'itoi, the mythic father of the Tohono O'odham and the Pima peoples.

Tohono O'odham country is desert, with no permanent stream or river. Summers are extremely hot and dry until the monsoon moisture that has slowly built up in the Gulf of Mexico travels northward in July and August to bring torrential downpours heralded by great dust storms and lightning displays. There is some light rain in winter as well. With so little water, farming was out of the question; the Tohono O'odham relied on wild foods for 75 percent of their diet. Because hunting and gathering were of such importance to their survival, the

## THE MAN IN THE MAZE

The symbol of the Tohono O'odham Nation is the Man in the Maze. Of the many variations that explain the design's meaning, the most common version tells of a desert people who forgot their spirituality. They stopped worshiping the Creator and no longer gave thanks for his bounty. They forgot their relationship to the animals and the plants, killing them without regard for their well-being.

Only I'itoi, Elder Brother, remained true to his beliefs. The Creator recognized I'itoi's true spirit and saved him from the flood sent to destroy humanity by placing I'itoi atop Baboquivari Peak, the sacred mountain of the Tohono O'odham.

After the floodwaters subsided, I'itoi helped create the ancestors of the Tohono O'odham and the Pima, teaching them the right way to live. I'itoi's spirit is thought to remain atop Baboquivari Peak.

The man at the top of the Man in the Maze design goes through many changes and turns in the maze of life. As each person goes deeper into the pattern over the course of his or her life, he or she becomes stronger and more understanding. The dark center of the design represents death, which the per-

*The Man in the Maze, painted here on a brick wall, is a common Tohono O'odham symbol.*

son realizes is coming. He or she is able to bypass death for a while by retreating to a small corner. After a period of cleansing and reflection, the person is restored to a state of harmony and accepts death peacefully.

*A photograph, taken around August 1915, shows Tohono O'odham women from San Xavier carrying pottery vessels filled with water. Woven head rings cushioned the round-bottomed jars.*

Tohono O'odham lived only part of the year in their villages near the fields that they cultivated with floodwater. In winter they sought out villages near permanent springs, or wells in the mountains. Their seminomadic life meant that the Tohono O'odham actually spent more time on the move than staying in the type of settled villages preferred by the ranchería farmers.

The traditional homes of the Tohono O'odham were round, grass-thatched, earth-covered houses with flat roofs. Later, they adopted Mexican-style adobe homes with nearby ramadas, which provided shade in the ovenlike heat of a Southwestern summer.

The Tohono O'odham constructed dikes and ditches to store runoff water when the rains came. They also practiced flash-flood farming, planting seeds after the first rains while the ground was still moist to obtain a small, quick harvest. From their winter villages in the mountains, the men hunted deer, bighorn sheep, javalinas (peccaries, piglike animals), and rabbits.

In summer, the blossoms of the giant saguaro cactus ripened into fruit that the women harvested, as some still do today. The Tohono O'odham ate this fruit fresh like candy or dried, or boiled it down into jam and syrup. They fermented some of the syrup to make a ritual wine for the annual summer rain ceremony.

It is easy to understand why one of the major Tohono O'odham ceremonies was the summer rain festival. In addition to their songs and prayers for rain, they participated in the ritual drinking of saguaro wine. They drank the wine until they could drink no more, hoping that the life-giving rain would likewise saturate the earth. They believed that the resulting altered state of consciousness purified their hearts and minds, thus encouraging the rain spirits.

Today, the Tohono O'odham no longer have to migrate to their winter villages because the United States government has drilled deep wells near their permanent villages. However, many of them must leave their homes to seek work because the reservation land cannot supply adequate food for their growing population. They rely on wage work and raising stock for their income. When the Tohono O'odham had to seek nonagricultural ways of making a living, the women began to sell their finely coiled baskets to tourists. Today they continue to weave close-coil and split-stitch baskets of yucca for the tourist market.

In contrast, the Pima, known as "The River People," traditionally practiced irrigation along the Salt and Gila Rivers. Their reliance on farming meant that the Pima could settle in more permanent villages, with agricultural products providing about 60 percent of their diet. They diverted river

*Juanita Ahil, a Tohono O'odham woman, collects saguaro fruit to make jam, candy, syrup, and wine for the rain ceremony.*

water into irrigation ditches so that they could farm corn, beans, and squash as well as the wheat and alfalfa that they acquired from the Spanish. They supplemented their diet with fish.

The Pima were such successful farmers that during the California gold rush they were able to sell their surplus crops to the forty-niners headed for the gold mines. However, once the white set-

*Tohono O'odham men and women dance during the summer rain ceremony in this painting by M. Chiago.*

## RANCHERÍA ARTS AND CRAFTS

The Pima and the Tohono O'odham traditionally made finely crafted coiled willow baskets. All the ranchería groups also made pottery. The Mohave, Yuma, Maricopa, and Cocopa produced painted dolls and long-necked jars.

The Yuman groups created beadwork necklaces that could extend over the shoulders. These designs in blue and white beads often resembled basketry designs. The Havasupai, Walapai, and Yavapai also made baskets.

Today, the Tohono O'odham probably produce more baskets than any other tribe in North America. They use bear grass and yucca to make coiled and split-stitched baskets. Many of their baskets are decorated with figures of animals, people, or saguaro cactus. They also make effigies of animals and people in basketry form and do some silverwork.

*An Ak-Chin O'odham girl proudly displays her coiled yucca basket.*

tlers dammed the Gila River for their agricultural needs, the Pima were no longer able to rely on farming and were forced to search for alternate ways to survive. A number of Pima people had to cut mesquite wood to earn a living. Today many depend upon wage work in nearby cities.

# THE YAQUI

A proud people, the Yaqui were such fierce warriors that they were able to defeat the Spanish forces in 1617 and establish relations with the Spaniards and their missionaries on their own terms. Much to the surprise of the Spaniards, those terms included the Yaqui request that Jesuit priests be sent to them.

For the next 120 years, there was a peaceful integration of Spanish and Yaqui culture in the eight Yaqui towns along the Rio Yaqui. The Yaqui were eager to learn new agricultural methods to increase their productivity. They also synthesized their aboriginal supernaturals with those of the Catholic system; for example, the Virgin Mary was integrated with the Yaqui supernatural, Our Mother, to honor the power of the Earth, trees, and flowers. They maintained a highly organized religious life centered around their cane shelter

churches where the Yaqui themselves—never Catholic priests—conducted the ceremonies.

By the 1730s, however, Spanish settlers began encroaching on Yaqui land situated along the river, leading to a revolt in which more than five thousand Indians were killed. As European settlers continued to move into Yaqui territory over the next century and a half, the Yaqui began to migrate away from their riverside towns. In 1887, the Mexican military began occupying many of their towns, and a number of Yaqui found their way north into Arizona, where they settled near Tucson. The military deported the Yaqui who still lived in their homeland to other parts of Mexico in an attempt to absorb them into the hacienda life of Yucatán and Oaxaca. (This was similar to the United States campaign of forced migration, the 1838 "Trail of Tears," which amounted to an attempt at genocide.) In 1906, the Yaqui were granted political asylum in the United States and celebrated their first Easter ceremony in Arizona. Most of them, however, owned no land but lived as squatters until Congress set aside 200 acres (81.4ha) southwest of Tucson for a Yaqui housing improvement program. In 1978, the United States government formally recognized the Yaqui as a native tribe and their land became a reservation.

# YAQUI EASTER

*A Yaqui Easter procession of Judases wearing helmet masks. Yaqui Easter ceremonies in Tucson, Arizona, are open to the public.*

In Yaqui communities in Tucson, the Yaqui people still celebrate the Lenten Season beginning on Ash Wednesday and continuing through Easter Sunday. It might appear that the Yaqui have adopted Catholicism, yet what they have really done is to modify Catholic symbols and beliefs into a unique Yaqui tradition.

Yaqui ceremonial life each year culminates in the ritual battle between good and evil that takes place at Easter. The purpose of the ceremony is to make the last days of Jesus real to the people by dramatizing his persecution and crucifixion.

The members of one Yaqui religious organization—the Judases—don helmet masks to represent Judas, the betrayer of Christ. The Judases, armed with wooden daggers and swords, are also known as devil clowns because they mock sacred institutions. They battle with the Matachinis, who are soldiers of the Virgin Mary, created to spread good influence by dancing in her honor. There are also little children dressed as angels, armed with the power of good, which is symbolized by flowers. Ultimately, the angels and the Matachinis defeat the evil Judases. The forces of good burn the Judases' helmet masks, delivering the community from their evil power.

Flowers are an important Yaqui symbol, for they represent the blood of Christ as it fell from the cross to mingle with the earth. By a miracle of Heaven, the Yaqui believe, Christ's blood was transformed into flowers. On the final procession of Easter Sunday, the flowers symbolize the moment when good triumphs.

# THE AGRICULTURAL BANDS

The Navajo and Apache peoples began moving southward from their ancestral Canadian homeland around the year 1300 and arrived in the Southwest about five hundred years ago. They were nomadic hunter-gatherers who learned how to farm, but hunting and wild-food gathering continued to be their main sources of food.

## THE NAVAJO

The Navajo Reservation is the largest Indian reservation in the United States and comprises 16 million acres (6.5 million ha). Stretching into parts of New Mexico, Arizona, and Utah, Navajo country is about the size of Vermont, New Hampshire, and Massachusetts combined.

The Four Corners area—where Arizona, New Mexico, Utah, and Colorado meet—has a great variety of vegetation. The Chuska and Lukachukai Mountains, which follow the New Mexico–Arizona state line, contain luxuriant forests of pine, spruce, fir, and aspen. Navajo Mountain rises 10,388 feet (3,166m). Below the peak lies the plateau region, a flat area covered with piñon, juniper, and sagebrush. The Navajo steppe lies still lower, a relatively flat land of yucca, grass, sagebrush, and greasewood. Two areas of Navajo country are true deserts: Monument Valley with its dramatic red sandstone buttes and towers, and the Painted Desert with its bright, banded clays.

The Navajo did not live in towns, but rather in isolated family groups. Each family lived in a rela-

*A Navajo woman, a grass hairbrush beside her, wraps her husband's hair in a traditional hair bundle as they sit in Monument Valley.*

*Left: A Navajo woman holds her granddaughter in front of their log hogan. Women provide the structure for Navajo society: a woman's property is passed down through her daughters, and all her children remain in her clan. Below: An old-style forked-stick hogan, a structure seldom seen on the reservation today.*

tively permanent camp located near their corn-fields. Women cultivated the fields or herded sheep while the men hunted deer. When the Navajo began herding sheep, they moved after the autumn harvest to a more substantial winter home with good pasturage for their flocks.

The Navajo lived, and often still live, in hogans, round, domed houses made of logs and chinked with mud. Built and blessed according to a sacred plan, hogans always face east, the direction of the rising sun. Family members usu-ally live near one another; when Navajo daughters marry, they bring their husbands home so they can help their in-laws.

The Navajo believe that by living with respect for all things, a person will enjoy health, prosperity, happiness, and peace. As the Navajo say, such a person "walks in beauty." But when someone fails to show the proper respect for life, he or she dis-rupts this balance and becomes ill. The solution is a ceremony to restore harmony, to reconnect the per-son to the forces of the universe. Thus, Navajo ceremonies focus on the curing of individual patients.

The Navajo system of cere-monies is very complex, with about twenty-four separate varieties of curing chants, some lasting as long as nine nights. The many songs, prayers,

*Navajo family members stand in front of their mud-chinked log hogan. When a woman married, her husband built their home near the bride's parents.*

sandpaintings, and ritual actions that are a part of a curing ceremony must be carried out in a prescribed sequence with word-perfect replication in order for the ceremony to be effective.

Each chant is a ritual drama that tells the story of the mythic journey of a hero or heroine who overcame great obstacles to receive healing. Sandpaintings, which are temporary images created from sand and other materials, depict the Holy People who were the characters in the accompanying myth. These vivid images can be as small as 12 inches (30.4cm) or as large as 20 feet (6m) in diameter. The chanter (who is usually, but not always, a man) and his helpers may take as long as ten hours to complete the detailed image. After its completion, the sandpainting is blessed, and the patient is sum-

moned to sit upon it. The healing power of the sand, as well as the power of the Holy People, is believed to penetrate the patient's body, bringing health and well-being and restoring balance. After the completion of various rituals, the patient stands up and the sand is taken to a spot north of the hogan, where it is respectfully allowed to return to the earth. If the ceremony is performed correctly, the patient overcomes his or her illness to once more "walk in beauty."

Navajo ceremonies continue to be performed today because the people have adapted so well to change. Part of the strength and vitality of their culture comes from their ability to borrow elements from other groups and to rework them into their own culture, with a distinctly Navajo result. When the ancestors of the Navajo made their way southward from Canada, they had to learn to survive in many different ecological and social environments. They succeeded because of their ability to adapt. After their arrival in the Southwest, they learned farming, animal husbandry, and weaving from the Pueblo Indians, and they adopted many important aspects of the Pueblo ceremonial system, as well.

The Spanish explorer Francisco Vásquez de Coronado (1510–1554) arrived in the Southwest in 1540, on a government-sponsored expedition to seek gold, new lands, and slave labor. The Navajo were, in a sense, the most fortunate of the Southwestern Indian peoples because they lived in relative isolation, not only from other Indians but also from each other. They did not live in villages, so the Spanish could not dominate them by moving in on their lands. Their isolation also protected them from the epidemics of measles, flu, and smallpox that killed thousands of Pueblo people. The Navajo were also known for their skills in war, and were able to capture Spanish horses, livestock, and steel weapons without fear of reprisals.

*A Navajo cowboy rides a bull at the Navajo Fair in Shiprock, New Mexico.*

Acquiring sheep and goats had a major impact upon the Navajo; by the late 1700s, the Navajo population began to increase because these animals furnished such a dependable food source. After the Navajo learned weaving from the Pueblo peoples, their fine blankets were in great demand.

In 1846, the United States took control of the Southwestern territories, promising settlers protec-

## NAVAJO COMMUNITY COLLEGE

Across the continent, tribally controlled colleges continue to change Indian lives by building both academic skills and pride in Native American cultures. The first tribal college, Navajo Community College, began classes in January 1969. Today, over two thousand students attend classes at the main campus in Tsaile, Arizona, or at the five community campuses.

Courses at Navajo Community College integrate typical college classes with Navajo courses. According to instructors David H. Begay amd Martha B. Bicktell, the personal finance course recognizes the Navajo custom of providing for the extended family.

The orientation of campus buildings also reflects traditional Navajo values: because the south is associated with daylight and the knowledge needed to make a living, this section of the campus houses the classrooms for professional and vocational subjects. The library, symbolic of sacred knowledge, is located on the north side of the campus, the

*A Native American church tipi and a Navajo hogan contrast with modern buildings at Navajo Community College.*

area of the hogan where a medicine bundle would be stored. The educational philosophy of Navajo Community College is based on Navajo tradition, whose guiding principle holds that human life is meant to exist in harmony with the natural world. Navajo-controlled education is an important step toward Indian sovereignty.

*Navajo women weep during a 1981 meeting in Cactus Valley, Arizona, on being forced to leave their homeland. "In our tongue," says one, "there is no word for relocation. To move away means to disappear and never be seen again."*

tion from Indians. Again, government misunderstandings of tribal organization set the stage for conflict and violence. The "chiefs" who signed treaties with the whites were only local headmen who led small groups of Navajo people. They had no power to make the rest of their people abide by the treaties.

Treaties and the construction of Fort Defiance in 1851 failed to decrease Navajo raids. When several punitive expeditions failed to stop the Navajo, Kit Carson and his soldiers began burning Navajo crops and homes in one of the most violent military campaigns in the history of North American Indians. Ute, Pueblo, and New Mexican volunteers also took revenge for previous Navajo raids by taking Navajo sheep and horses, killing Navajo men, capturing Navajo women and children for slaves, burning their hogans, and destroying their crops. A brutal winter sealed the defeat of the Navajo warriors.

The people then faced the horror of the Long Walk—an arduous trek of 300 miles (480km)—to Fort Sumner, New Mexico, where they were imprisoned from 1864 to 1868. They were a proud, independent people accustomed to moving freely across the great spaces of their beloved homeland. Suddenly they had become captives confined within a limited area, dependent upon the government. Not only did they suffer the emotional and spiritual anguish of exile, but many of them died because of insufficient food, recurring crop failure, and disease.

Congress finally realized that keeping the Navajo imprisoned was simply costing the federal government too much money. They agreed to let the Navajo go home. Although it took them a long time to recover, the Navajo population eventually outgrew the resources of their reservation. By the 1930s, their sheep had destroyed much of the ground cover, leading to wind and soil erosion. To prevent further overgrazing, the government began the Stock Reduction Program, which many Navajos remember with the same sadness as Fort Sumner. Navajos measured their wealth in sheep; sheep were part of their identity. During the enforced stock reduction, many Navajos died of what they called *ch'ééná*, sadness for a way of life that is gone forever.

# NAVAJO CHURRO SHEEP

About four hundred years ago, the Spaniard Juan de Oñate (first governor of New Mexico Territory) brought churro sheep—known for their long, coarse wool and unique four-horned rams—to the Rio Grande Valley in New Mexico. The churro sheep were perfect for the needs of the Navajo: the animals were resistant to disease, reproduced easily, and produced wool that was ideal for hand-weaving. Navajo raiding parties took the churro into what is now western New Mexico, southern Utah, and northern Arizona, where they developed large flocks by the late 1500s.

When the Navajo were exiled to Fort Sumner, their sheep were destroyed. The government issued them sheep upon their return to their homeland; however, these sheep were a mixture of Merino, Rambouillet, and churro stock. The crossbred Merino lambs were too large for the small Navajo churro ewes to bear safely, and the wool their offspring produced was too greasy and too wavy for fine Navajo weaving.

Later, during the Stock Reduction Program, government representatives did not allow the Navajo to choose which of the different sheep breeds they would save. Herds were killed indiscriminately and many valuable churros were slaughtered.

In 1977, the Navajo Sheep Project began an effort to rescue churro sheep, which are still on the endangered list of the American Minor Breeds Conservancy. Since 1982, Navajo Sheep Project staff members have been working with the Navajo to provide training in animal breeding, sheep and range management, and programs in the shearing, preparing, and packaging of wool.

*Above: Traditional Navajo blankets. Left: A Navajo weaver. Navajo legend says that Spider Woman instructed Navajo women how to weave on a loom with crosspoles of sky and earth cords, warp sticks of sun rays, and healds of rock crystal and sheet lightning.*

# ARTS AND CRAFTS OF THE AGRICULTURAL BANDS

Although the Navajo learned weaving from Pueblo men, Navajo women are the weavers in their culture. They began by copying the simple banded designs of the Pueblos in their blankets. Later, regional styles developed in different parts of the large reservation. When the transcontinental railroad was built in the 1890s, linking the reservation to the East Coast, lightweight clothing blankets gave way to heavy rugs for the tourist market. Although weaving generally is not profitable, some women continue to weave finely made rugs.

Navajo silverwork is one of the best-known Native American crafts today. They learned how to work silver from the Mexicans in the 1850s and began producing silver jewelry in the 1870s. They soon adapted the designs into Navajo forms and, just as they had with weaving, soon surpassed the quality of their teachers' products. Navajo designs tend to be fairly heavy, set with large pieces of turquoise.

The Navajo still make a simple, glossy brown pottery. Their red, black, and white baskets are often actually made by the Paiute; there are many Navajo taboos associated with this type of basket making because the baskets are used in Navajo ceremonials.

Commercial sandpaintings glued onto boards have become a popular art form in recent years. For these paintings, artists either alter sacred designs or depict subject matter that would never be considered sacred.

Some Apache women still weave baskets. The Western Apache, in particular, are known for their coiled baskets of fine quality. These baskets are often decorated with whirling linear patterns, star designs, or human or animal figures in black and red on a tan background.

*Above: Navajo silverwork with its distinctive large pieces of turquoise. Left: A Navajo sandpainter demonstrates his technique in depicting Fringe Mouths from the Nightway.*

*An Apache woman stands in the doorway of her wickiup, next to a twined pack basket with buckskin fringe. A woven basket water-proofed with piñon gum sits at lower left.*

# THE APACHE

There were many Apache groups scattered across the Southwest. The Lipan depended primarily on hunting and gathering and raiding ranches for cattle from their eastern New Mexico and west Texas homeland. The Western Apache of east-central Arizona farmed more than other Apaches. The Jicarilla Apache of northern New Mexico farmed and hunted buffalo. The Kiowa-Apache lived with the Kiowa of the Great Plains. The Chiricahua of southern Arizona and New Mexico reared great warriors, Cochise and Geronimo among them, who achieved fame well beyond their tribal borders. The

Mescalero lived in south-central New Mexico and got their name from the mescal (agave) plant which, traditionally, was an essential part of their diet. With piñon sticks, the women chopped off the huge crowns of the mescal plant and roasted them in a cooking pit.

When the Spanish arrived during their 1540 expedition, the Apache were one of the groups they encountered. Pedro Casteneda, Coronado's narrator, described the Apache as intelligent, tall, well-built, friendly, and kind people. The Spanish soon discovered, however, that they could not bend this proud people to their will. The Spanish promised peace, but as various leaders vied for power, they did not keep their promise. In response, Apache raiders attacked the settlements.

Over the next three hundred years of uneasy cohabitation in the Southwest, the slave trade increased hostilities: the Pawnee Indians of the Plains raided the Apache camps for women and children, while the Apache raiders sold captured Pawnees to the Spanish. The Spanish also sold Apache women and children to Mexicans. In contrast, when the Mescalero captured or bought a woman, they married her to one of their warriors; the couple's children became full members of the tribe.

When the United States took over the Southwest in 1846, the Apache raiders simply switched their attacks to representatives of the government instead of individuals. When Susan Shelby Magoffin accompanied her husband to the area from 1846 to 1847, she wrote that some Mescalero came in to drive off "twenty yoke of oxen belonging only to the government." The Apaches wanted food; they did not harm anyone.

By the 1860s and 1870s, the relationship between the whites and Mexicans and the Apache people had deteriorated sharply; torture was commonly committed upon prisoners on all sides. The Mexicans were known to offer peace, only to slaughter Apaches when they accepted the offer.

When Confederate troops controlled the area around El Paso, Texas, during the Civil War, they, too, fought the Apache.

Eventually, the government burned the Mescalero out of their homes just as they had the Navajo. Although these two groups were not traditionally friendly, in 1863 the government imprisoned the Mescalero with the Navajo at Fort Sumner, New Mexico.

During this period, Cochise and Geronimo, the great warriors of the Chiricahua Apache, fought fiercely for their people. From their stronghold in the Dragoon Mountains, they conducted raids for livestock and sent war parties to avenge deaths suffered at the hands of their enemies. All Apache groups were respected warriors: their complete knowledge of the desert and mountain terrain, along with their remarkable powers of endurance and resourcefulness, enabled them to attack without warning. Indeed, General George Crook described the Apache as the finest light cavalry in all of North America. In 1872, Cochise signed a peace treaty; his band of Chiricahua remained at peace until after his death in 1874. Geronimo, however, fought on with a handful of warriors. After a series of surrenders and escapes, Geronimo finally surrendered in 1886.

*Apache prisoners on their way to prison rest beside a Southern Pacific Railway car near the Nueces River, Texas, September 10, 1886. Geronimo is in the front row, third from the right; his son sits on his left.*

# LIFE TODAY: THE APACHE FEMALE PUBERTY CEREMONY

*Left: Apache Aleshia during her puberty ceremony. Above: An Apache girl stands beside her godmother during the pollen blessing. The abalone shell on her forehead identifies her with White Painted Woman; her cane symbolizes old age.*

When Apache and Navajo girls come of age, their people still celebrate their passage into womanhood in what is probably the most elaborate puberty ceremony in North America. Not only is this a celebration of each girl's individual womanhood, but it is also a celebration of ongoing life for all of their people. For the Mescalero Apache, the Holy Men/Singers not only sing the women into their adult roles; they also sing tribal history. Their songs reaffirm the existence and identity of the people as they reenact events from the beginning of time.

Several girls between the ages of twelve and fourteen are launched into womanhood in an elaborate four-day ceremonial rich in the symbolism of important values. A carefully chosen Godmother directs each girl. The Godmother embodies the values and sense of responsibility that the girl hopes to attain. The older woman is not related to the girl by blood, yet this ceremony links them in a continuing relationship as close as kinship. It is a way of establishing lifelong bonds of mutual aid outside the boundaries of family, thus knitting the community more closely together.

The abalone shell placed on the girl's forehead symbolizes her identification with White Shell Woman or White Painted Woman. The Navajo call this beloved deity Changing Woman, and she represents the powers of the changing Earth to renew itself through the seasons, the giver of all life.

The girl is blessed with the symbol of the Creator's generosity—cattail pollen from tule rushes—and she wears a dress of golden buckskin. The cane in her hand represents the old age that she hopes to reach by following the right ideals. The cane is adorned with oriole feathers to symbolize the even temperament that will allow her to get along well with others, and eagle feathers to represent the gray color of her hair at old age, another hope for long life. In contrast to the puberty ceremony of the California Indians, in which girls lie in isolation because of their "impurity," the Apache and Navajo celebrate a woman's physical strength and her contribution to her people. An important part of the ceremony comes when the girls run, symbolizing strength and endurance for themselves and for their tribe.

Generosity is another important value that is evident in the massive food giveaways of the puberty ceremony. As a Mescalero singer told anthropologist Claire Farrer, "The four laws of our people are honesty, generosity, pride, and bravery....It is out of generosity that a man sees the world. He cannot be proud if he is not generous, as he has nothing to be proud for and brave for....Honesty has no basis without generosity."

# HOPI ORAL TRADITION AND ARCHAEOLOGY

The Hopi believe that when their people were first created, Ma'saw, the guardian of this, the Fourth World, gave them the responsibility of cultivating and caring for the earth. The ancient Hopi clans began a spiritual quest to find their destiny and their rightful place at the center of the universe. Priests served as their guides, interpreting supernatural phenomena and natural events like earthquakes as spiritual signs. Eventually, they arrived at the Hopi mesas. The ruins and potsherds they had left behind in their migrations provided physical evidence that they had blessed the land with their spiritual stewardship, fulfilling their promise to Ma'saw. Their ancestors did not abandon these places, say the Hopi; instead, they continue to watch over them as spiritual guardians.

The Hopi Tribe and archaeologists from the Arizona State University are developing a large excavation project in the Tonto Basin of central Arizona. Together, they are trying to integrate Hopi clan history, which is passed down in stories from generation to generation, with the artifacts found there. According to the Hopi, nine clans once lived within the Tonto Basin region. Hopi elders, working with archaeologists, have identified the uses of some ancient ritual artifacts. By sharing their history, the Hopi are helping scientists to learn more from the archaeological record, which, in turn, is helping the Hopi to better understand their tribal history.

*The exterior walls of Hopi dwellings are constructed of stone slabs supported by heavy beams. Because wood is so scarce in the Hopi area, when a Hopi builds a new home, he often salvages the beams from the old house.*

*Above: When the Spanish arrived in the Southwest, there were about ninety pueblos; today only thirty are occupied. Pueblos like this one in New Mexico lie along the Rio Grande; other pueblos are found farther west. Below: Pueblos are usually made of adobe, a type of clay that is often mixed with earth and straw.*

## THE VILLAGE FARMERS

The ruins of the cliff-dwelling Anasazi people—ancestors of today's Pueblo peoples—are scattered through the canyons of the Four Corners area of Utah, Colorado, Arizona, and New Mexico. This is an area of sandstone plateaus with narrow canyons and valleys that experience great extremes of temperature—burning, hot summers and cold, snowy winters. "Pueblo" refers both to a village and to the Indian peoples who live in that type of village.

By 300 B.C., the Anasazi were such successful farmers that they were able to live in settled villages with two- to four-storied apartmentlike buildings and ceremonial structures called kivas. They made elaborate pottery, the remains of which allow archaeologists to

date the various periods of their history. At the end of the fourteenth century, the Pueblo peoples began abandoning their early sites, probably because of drought. When the Spanish explorers arrived in the sixteenth century, they found the Pueblo peoples living where they are today—along the Rio Grande in northern New Mexico and in isolated villages in western New Mexico and the Hopi mesas of northern Arizona.

# POPÉ

Long before the arrival of the Spanish, the ancestors of the Pueblo people lived along the Rio Grande in what is now New Mexico. In their settled villages, they wove fine cotton cloth, made pottery, and practiced irrigation farming. Their spiritual beliefs and practices provided the foundation for their lives.

The Pueblo way of life was threatened when Spanish colonists and priests established a territorial capital at Santa Fe in 1609. (Today it is the oldest state capital in the United States.) The Spanish made the Indians pay taxes in the form of cloth, corn, or labor. They forbade native ceremonies and practices and renamed Pueblo villages after Catholic saints. The Indians responded by adopting the appearances of Catholicism while secretly continuing to practice native ceremonies in their kivas.

The Spanish ruthlessly exploited Indian labor; they also whipped and executed native religious leaders. When Spanish domination became intolerable, Popé (?–1692), a medicine man from the Tewa Pueblo of San Juan, enlisted the aid of virtually every Pueblo to lead them in rebellion. Imprisoned by the Spanish, then later released, Popé planned the Pueblo Revolt. In 1680, the Pueblos under Popé attacked, driving out the Spanish and regaining control of their country for the next twelve years. After Popé's death in 1692, Spanish rule was reinstated, but under somewhat more humane conditions with greater freedom of religion for the Pueblo peoples.

# GROWING UP ZUNI

Like many native young people, Zuni teenagers are torn between the non-Indian world and the Zuni world. They play basketball until dark, shooting hoops suspended from adobe walls. Then they go inside for a traditional dinner of steamed tamales, beef stew, and Zuni bread baked in a beehive oven.

Zunis try to pass down traditional stories from grandparents to grandchildren, but most children no longer learn the Zuni language. The connecting link between the generations continues to grow weaker. The Zuni Senior Citizen Center is trying to strengthen that link. Each morning senior men and women visit classrooms as foster grandparents, sharing stories and school activities with preschool and elementary school children.

Still, as the children approach adulthood, they have far more opportunities to enter the non-Zuni world than did previous generations. Most high school students at Zuni will be the first in their families who will be able to go to college. Meanwhile, there is a diminishing need for the traditional Zuni jobs of herding and jewelry making that supported their parents and grandparents.

Success for a Zuni young person is difficult to define because it means so many things to different people. To the younger generation, it may mean leaving the reservation to work as a diesel mechanic; to traditional Zuni grandparents, it means understanding Zuni language and culture and participating in ceremonies. Growing up Zuni in today's world is a challenge as young people try to find the balance between their obligations to their ancestors and their place in the larger world.

*Left: Bread is baked inside a beehive oven. Below: A Zuni girl, wearing a rainbow tablita on her head, dances in Santa Fe with her two male companions.*

Despite their many cultural similarities—settled village life, farming, pottery making, and a rich ceremonial life that emphasizes weather control—the Pueblo peoples speak a number of different languages. This means that a Zuni cannot understand the speech of a Hopi, nor can a Keresan-speaker from Cochiti communicate with a Tewa-speaker from Tesuque.

Just as the differences between the Havasupai and the Walapai, and the Pima and the Tohono O'odham resulted from access to a river, so did the differences between the Eastern Pueblos and the Western Pueblos. The Eastern Pueblos—Santa Ana, San Felipe, Santo Domingo, Cochiti, Zia, Jemez, Sandia, Isleta, Picuris, Taos, Tesuque, Nambe, Pojoaque, San Ildefonso, Santa Clara, and San Juan—built their villages along the Rio Grande and its tributaries in order to use the river to irrigate the fields they planted in riverbeds. The peoples of the Western Pueblos of Zuni, Hopi, Hano, Acoma, and Laguna had to rely on the runoff from seasonal rains for their crops, which were planted strategically at the mouths of washes.

The Pueblo peoples raised corn, beans, squash, cotton, and tobacco. From the Spanish, they acquired wheat, melons, chili peppers, and fruit trees. They hunted deer, antelope, and rabbits as well.

Unlike the Navajo, whose ceremonials focused on the health of individuals, the Pueblo peoples emphasized community well-being. Their ceremonies were concerned with controlling the weather, healing illness, achieving success in warfare, controlling plants and animals, and ensuring village harmony.

The Western Pueblos emphasized weather control, especially rain production, over any of the other concerns in their ceremonials. With no permanent source of water, they attempted in their rituals to persuade nature to be more bountiful. Among their religious practices is the Kachina cult.

Kachinas are supernatural beings who are vaguely considered to be ancestral spirits. They are believed to have the power to bring rain and confer

## TAOS BLUE LAKE

In 1906, without consulting the Taos pueblo, the United States government put Taos Blue Lake and 50,000 adjacent acres (20,350ha) under the jurisdiction of the Forest Service. For the next sixty-five years, Taos government officials and a nationwide coalition of Indians and non-Indians struggled to regain control of Blue Lake and the surrounding land. Querino Romero, governor of the Taos pueblo for three terms, and his wife, Daisy Romero, led the fight for the return of this sacred land, the place of emergence for the Taos Indians. The United States government returned the land in 1971, the first time that they had given back a large, valuable tract of land to an Indian tribe. Each year, the people of Taos pueblo walk the 15 to 20 miles (24 to 32km) to Blue Lake, where they pray for the welfare and harmony of all people.

general well-being. Best known among the Hopi, these supernatural beings are believed to arrive in December for the winter solstice and leave in June to return to their homes atop San Francisco Peaks, near Flagstaff, Arizona. During their dances, priests of the Kachina cult wear masks and impersonate the gods; they believe that they temporarily give up their human spirit and become the spirit whose mask they wear while dancing.

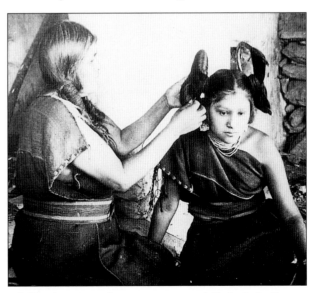

*A Hopi woman dresses a young girl's hair in the butterfly/squash-blossom hairdo of a maiden. Once married, the girl will wear her hair in braids.*

Kachinas can also take the form of Kachina dolls, which are carved, painted likenesses of these beings. The Kachina impersonators give the dolls to children to teach them about the spirits. Children are then initiated into the Kachina cult between seven and ten years of age. That is when they learn that the Kachina impersonators are their fellow villagers and friends. From then on, boys can participate in ceremonies and girls can help with ceremonial preparations.

The Kachinas take many forms: ogres who threaten disobedient children, birds similar to the eagle, animals such as the wolf, and even natural phenomena such as clouds, prized for their ability to bring rain. Ceremonial clowns also play a vital role in the rituals, for the Hopi believe that human laughter and smiles are sacred. The clowns go down ladders headfirst, toppling over themselves, illustrating the human tendency to accomplish tasks in the most difficult way; they also imitate members of the audience. The clowns, say the Hopi, keep us from taking ourselves too seriously, teaching us how to laugh at ourselves.

## NATIVE SEEDS/SEARCH

The Native peoples of the Southwest were expert farmers who created many new varieties of plants. Native Seeds/SEARCH is a nonprofit seed conservation organization established to preserve the wide variety of wild plants and crops grown and harvested by these skilled farmers. (SEARCH is Southwestern Endangered Arid-land Resource Clearing House.) For the last ten years, this group has maintained a seedbank of plants representing the agricultural achievements of many tribes.

The Hopi are known for the varieties of corn they developed, especially the blue corn. The Havasupai grow many field and tree crops; their peaches are especially renowned. The Hopi and Havasupai have long shared cultural and trade ties, including the exchange of seeds. Traditionally, the Indians of the New Mexico Pueblos had many crop varieties: hot and mild chilies, squash, and melons. The Navajo now have the largest acreage in native crops of any tribe in the United States. They and, to a lesser extent, their Apache cousins, specialize in the raising of corn, one of their sacred plants. The River Yumans began farming the floodplains along the Gila and lower Colorado Rivers around A.D. 800. The Tohono O'odham and Pima have developed some of the most drought-resistant, heat-tolerant, and alkali-adapted crops in the world. Traditionally, they raised sixty-day corn, tepary beans, and striped cushaw squash that they could produce during the brief, torrential summer rains.

Gary Nabhan, one of the founders of Native Seeds/SEARCH, explained that there are several important

*Part of the agricultural heritage of Southwestern tribes including several varieties of corn and peppers preserved by Native Seeds/SEARCH.*

reasons to preserve this gardening heritage. Many of the wild and cultivated plants native to the Americas are unusually rich in the kind of complex carbohydrates that can prevent or control diabetes, the number one health problem among contemporary Native Americans. These plants also serve as the primary resource for plant breeding programs to increase the commercial crops' resistance to insects, diseases, and droughts and freezes. For example, Havasupai Indian sunflowers were recently discovered to be the only kind of sunflowers that are 100 percent resistant to a rust strain that is devastating all sunflower hybrids in the United States and Canada. Such native crop diversity strengthens all major food crops, ensuring future stability in the global food supply.

# ARTS AND CRAFTS OF THE VILLAGE FARMERS

**M**any Pueblo women continue to make beautiful pottery in distinctive styles. Some Pueblos, such as Taos and Picuris, make only unpainted tan pottery with flecks of glittering mica. Cochiti and Santo Domingo make cream pottery with black designs of geometric patterns and birds. The thinnest pottery is produced at Acoma and is decorated with birds and flowers or allover geometric patterns. In 1919, María and Julián Martínez, potters at the San Ildefonso pueblo, began using dull black paint on polished black ware. Zuni pottery has large designs painted in brown with touches of red on a white background; a favorite motif is a deer with a red "heart line," which symbolizes the spirit of life within the animal.

Hopi pottery was revived in 1900, when Nampeyo, a Hano woman from First Mesa, copied fine prehistoric pottery found near her village. She developed a style based on the ancient Sikyatki ware, with stylized birds and kachinas painted in black, orange, and white designs on a cream, white, or dark red background.

The finest Pueblo baskets are made at Hopi: Third Mesa women are known for their colorful wicker baskets, while the basket makers of Second Mesa make bright coiled baskets. The weaving of cloth was man's work in Pueblo culture. Hopi men continue to weave ceremonial garments of cotton and wool in the form of kilts, belts, sashes, and wedding robes. It is the responsibility of the groom's father to weave the bride's wedding robe while a woman from her family weaves a special basket for the groom.

Several pueblos made small wooden dolls to represent Kachinas. The carving and painting of these figures has become increasingly popular at Hopi for sale to tourists.

Some Pueblo groups are known for their silver jewelry. Hopi silverwork uses cutout silver soldered over sheet silver with a recessed design that is blackened to heighten the effect. Zuni jewelry uses inlays of turquoise, jet, or red spiny oyster, or many small turquoise sets.

*Top: A turtle coiled plaque created by Hopi weaver Evelyn Pela. Left: Jemez potter Evelyn Vigil decorates her pottery before firing it. Pueblo potters still create their pots by hand with a coil technique, rather than by using a potter's wheel.*

# INDIANS TODAY

Over a century ago, General George Armstrong Custer said, "We behold [the Indian] now on the verge of extinction...and soon he will be talked of as a noble race who once existed but have passed away." Despite such dire predictions, Native Americans have done anything but disappear. Today, in the United States and Canada, there are nearly two million Native Americans.

After the end of the Indian wars in the 1880s, the United States government tried to force Native peoples to assimilate. In 1824, the Bureau of Indian Affairs was established—within the War Department. Not until 1849 was the Bureau of Indian Affairs moved to the Department of the Interior.

Government officials, hoping to "civilize" the Indians by making them into farmers, broke up tribal lands and allotted 160 acres (65.1ha) to the head of each household and smaller tracts to individuals. This program was named the General Allotment Act, or simply the Dawes Act, after Senator Henry Dawes of Massachusetts, who triumphantly led its passage through Congress in 1887. One of the most significant laws in American Indian history, the Allotment Act took 86 million reservation acres (35 million ha) from Native Americans, two-thirds of all their holdings. The land that remained after allotment was opened to white settlement.

*Opposite: Annual pow-wows have become a growing trend among Native Americans, who travel great distances to take part in dancing and inter-tribal singing contests. Left: In 1907, a Presbyterian missionary bought these Indian skulls for $30, later selling them to the Heye Foundation (now part of the National Museum of the American Indian, Smithsonian Institution) in New York. These Sioux men, members of the Water Busters Clan, were instrumental in securing the return of their sacred relics.*

Such government programs assumed that Native Americans were in the process of vanishing, of slowly assimilating into white culture so that, in time, there would be no Indians. As time has proved, nothing could be further from the truth.

Education was another avenue for forced assimilation. Missionaries flocked to reservations to convert Indians. Government officials captured unwilling children and took them to boarding schools where they remained separate from their homes and families. Indian children were not allowed to speak their own languages and were often beaten if they disobeyed.

One unexpected effect of this system was that because of the mixing of various tribes, many Native Americans developed a sense of themselves as Indians beyond their tribal affiliations—a pan-Indian identity. When whites had first arrived, Indians were living in small tribal groups, each of which thought of everyone outside their group, even other Indians, as separate peoples. Indeed, North America's native peoples had no sense of being "Indian." The names that groups have for themselves reflect this: the Cherokees call themselves a phrase that translates as "Real Human Beings" while the Iroquois refer to themselves as "Men of Men."

*Left: Sioux boys arrive at Carlisle Indian School, Pennsylvania, October 5, 1879. The staff at Carlisle soon cut their hair and replaced their traditional clothing with school uniforms like those worn by the Omaha boys in the photo below.*

*John Collier, commissioner of Indian Affairs, poses with Blackfeet leaders in 1934 at Rapid City, South Dakota, where they were meeting to discuss the Wheeler-Howard Act.*

In boarding schools, contact with tribal peoples from so many groups made the students aware of their identity as Indians. They realized that they belonged to a much wider group than their own individual tribe and that they were not alone in their struggle for equality. By joining together, they found comfort in each other and in their shared identity.

An unexpected result of white attempts to end Native American religious practices is the Native American Church, founded in 1918, which combines tenets of traditional Indian religion and fundamental Christianity. It is the most widespread religion among Indians in the United States today. The most important sacrament is the eating of the peyote button, a hallucinogenic cactus, in order to induce contact with the supernatural; this aspect of the religion has created considerable controversy with the United States government.

Despite the U.S. government's desire to assimilate Indians into American culture, it was not until 1924 that Congress enacted a statute to prove citizenship for all Indians. Later, questioning the wisdom of earlier policies, John Collier, commissioner of Indian Affairs from 1933 to 1946, tried to reverse the disastrous program of forced assimilation by expanding tribal land holdings and encouraging self-government on the reservations. The Indian Reorganization Act of 1934, also called the Wheeler-Howard Act, stopped all land allotment to whites, and granted development aid to enable tribes to form corporations to manage their own resources. The freedom to practice traditional religion was one of the most significant features of this act. This meant that tribal elders no longer had to hide in order to perform their sacred rituals. Native American spirituality could now be practiced in freedom without fear of punishment.

World War II brought many Indians into an experience of the broader world. Members of many tribes fought for their country. Among them, over 3,600 Navajos served in World War II. Of these men, 420 were Code Talkers, who baffled the Japanese with some four hundred code words based on the Navajo language. Navajo Code Talkers played a vital role in the monthlong battle for Iwo Jima. One (non-Indian) officer even said, "Without the Navajos the Marines would never have taken Iwo Jima."

Ira Hayes, a Pima Indian, helped raise the American flag on Iwo Jima; he was featured in one of the most popular photographs of World War II, which became a symbol of American patriotism. However, as with many black soldiers, when Indians returned from the war, they were faced with the same level of discrimination and economic hardship that they had hoped to leave behind. Many, including Ira Hayes, faced a postwar life of such despair that they succumbed to alcoholism.

*Pima Indian Ira Hayes is second from left, helping raise the American flag on Iwo Jima during World War II.*

*Onondaga Indian Horace Cook fights toxic waste disposal on tribal land. The waste industry targets reservations because environmental regulations are less strict on tribal land.*

In November 1944, nearly one hundred representatives from more than forty tribes met in Denver to form the first all-Indian nationwide organization, the National Congress of American Indians. NCAI joined the effort to establish the Indian Claims Commission in 1946. This commission provided a way for tribes to file claims directly against the United States government for land. Until this commission was created, tribes had to obtain a special Act of Congress in order to sue the government. The government, which thought such an organization would be temporary, was overwhelmed by the enormous number of Indian land claims that flooded the commission.

In 1953, "termination," the elimination of expensive federal services to the tribes, became the official government policy. The Menominee of

Wisconsin were pressured into termination in 1961 with disastrous results. To increase their taxable income, they were forced to automate their sawmill, which threw people out of work and onto welfare. Within a decade the Menominee went from being relatively self-sufficient to living in one of the ten most financially depressed counties in the United States.

Relocation was another disastrous aspect of termination. The government provided one-way transportation to a large city and helped the relocated family find jobs and housing. For a small handful this shift to the city was beneficial, but for most Indians, it meant only an exchange of rural poverty for urban poverty.

In 1961 Indians held a historic conference at the University of Chicago: five hundred Indians

*Bear Forgets (right), a Sioux in full regalia, celebrates "Liberation Day" on Alcatraz Island, May 31, 1970 ,
during the Indians of All Tribes' nineteen-month occupation of the island. Alcatraz is now a national park.*

from seventy United States tribes attended, as well as Indian observers from Canada and Mexico. One result of the conference was the formation of the National Indian Youth Council. Today this group has over 46,000 members in the United States and actively promotes Indian cultural and political issues.

In 1964 the National Congress of American Indians cosponsored a conference on Indian poverty. Native Americans had (and continue to have) the nation's lowest annual income and life expectancy rates and the highest rates of unemployment, suicide, alcoholism, and infant mortality of all ethnic groups in North America.

With the establishment of the Office of Economic Opportunity (OEO), tribes finally received access to funds, agencies, and programs. For the first time, tribes were deeply involved in projects under a variety of federal agencies, instead of only through the Bureau of Indian Affairs.

OEO programs have since provided many opportunities in various areas. The Lummi of western Washington built a unique sea farm based on aquaculture in Lummi Bay, where they could harvest salmon, trout, and shellfish. In Minnesota, the Red Lake Chippewa, and in Arizona, the Gila River Pima and Maricopa used funds to improve reservation housing. Head Start (for preschool children),

Upward Bound (for college-oriented students), and Indian-controlled schools helped prepare Indians for higher education. School curriculums began to include bilingual programs, and courses in Indian history and art. High-level jobs in federal agencies and on the reservations themselves opened to Native Americans.

However, economic and health problems remain serious challenges. A new generation of Indian activists have tried to bring these problems to the conscience of all Americans. In 1964 Indians in Washington staged "fish-ins" on the Puyallup, Nisqually, and Green Rivers to protest restrictions on Indian fishing rights guaranteed by federal treaty. A group calling themselves Indians of All Tribes occupied Alcatraz in San Francisco Bay from November 1969 to June 1971.

In 1972 the American Indian Movement (AIM), a group of militant activists, took over the Bureau of Indian Affairs offices in Washington, D.C., to demand improved programs for Indians.

Indian activism culminated in a major confrontation in 1973 at Wounded Knee in South Dakota on the Pine Ridge Reservation. This was the same site at which the United States Cavalry in 1890 massacred 150 to 300 Sioux for their participation in the Ghost Dance Movement. For seventy-one days, armed AIM members held Wounded Knee, facing a military force of a size that had not been seen on United States soil since the Civil War.

## CANADIAN INDIANS

Historically, the Canadian government has taken a different approach than the United States government in the treatment of Native peoples. Rather than concentrating the Indians on reservations far from their original homelands, the Canadian policy was to allow them to remain, in widely scattered bands, on their traditional lands. Although the Canadian government had economic reasons for this policy—it was cheaper to support the Indians who retained their traditional hunting economy—Canadian Indians were nevertheless able to preserve more of their culture.

This more humane approach was feasible because, compared to the United States, Canada had a relatively small white population. South of the border, settlers soon filled all usable space; by 1800 the United States government had made available to settlers most of the land that had once belonged to Native Americans. The Canadian approach, however, was based on a more respectful colonial policy developed first by the French and later by the English. The Native leader Louis Riel (1844–1885), who was part Indian and part Metis (of both Indian and French ancestry), actually served in Parliament before running afoul of the law. After the government put down an 1885 rebellion led by Riel in Saskatchewan (for which he was convicted as a traitor and hanged), instead of trying to intimidate the other Native leaders, the government thanked those who had remained loyal by inviting them to meet with Canada's prime minister.

However, although Canadian policy was somewhat more humane, Native peoples in Canada lost as much land as those in the United States; in 1923, only six million acres (2.4 million ha) remained under Canadian Indian control. In 1982, Canada finally recognized the constitutional existence of "aboriginal and treaty rights."

After many years of negotiation, an Inuit (Eskimo) land claim has been settled. In 1999, Nunavut (Inuit for "our home") Territory will be established. The 733,591 square miles (1,900,000 sq km) of Nunavut Territory will comprise 14,622 square miles (37,870 sq km) of Inuit-owned land with mineral rights; 122,769 square miles (317,971 sq km) of Inuit-owned land without mineral rights; and crown (government) lands. This agreement includes a capital transfer of over $1 billion to the Inuit people over the course of fourteen years. The government will also put $13 million into a trust fund to train and create jobs for the Inuit. Inuit leaders are also pushing for a five-year residency requirement for voters so that Nunavet is protected against boom-or-bust resource development. Although other Native groups around the country continue to press outstanding land claims, this legislation is an important step forward for Native Americans in Canada.

*Above: Indians stand guard outside the Sacred Heart Catholic Church during the siege at Wounded Knee, South Dakota. Long delays by the government in addressing Indian grievances led the American Indian Movement (AIM) to seize Wounded Knee for three months in 1973. Left: Riders follow the Chief Big Foot Trail in December 1990 on the one hundredth anniversary of the massacre at Wounded Knee.*

By the time federal officials had negotiated a with-drawal, two Indian militants were dead and a marshal was paralyzed. Wounded Knee clouded the issues with media displays—the radical Indian movement coincided with "radical" youth activity across America—but it did prove that Indians had neither vanished nor assimilated into white culture. This confrontation inspired whites and Indians alike to look for new solutions.

The nineties have seen some new solutions to poverty and health problems, a cultural flowering of powwows and festivals all over North America, and even burgeoning wealth for a few, isolated tribes. However, many challenges remain to be faced by the young Indians of today: unemploy-ment and poverty remain rampant on reserva-tions. One solution to these issues may be Indian gaming: some reservation casinos take in as much

*Bella dancers compete at a powwow, a growing tradition. Dance remains an expression and celebration of Indian spirituality and community.*

## THE STRUGGLE FOR CANADIAN INDIAN IDENTITY

On July 11, 1990, police tried to dismantle a road-block that the Mohawk Indians of Quebec had built to prevent the expansion of a golf course on land they regarded as their own. Municipal authorities in the resort town of Oka on the Ottawa River 20 miles (32km) west of Montreal brought in police during the seventy-eight-day standoff. Eventually, the authorities backed down and the golf course was never built.

However, anger still resonates among the 1,500 Kanesatake (Mohawk) Indians. Several of them told Clyde Farnsworth of *The New York Times* that the government intends to "keep the natives down" and "never to settle with us." In reaction to the Oka crisis, the Canadian govern-ment established the Royal Commission on Aboriginal Peoples. Their findings were grim: high suicide and crime rates, alcohol and drug addiction, and economic despair characterize the lives of many of Canada's 400,000 tribal people. The commission's report, to be published next winter, is expected to call for self-government as a way to increase self-esteem and economic self-reliance.

The native peoples of Canada are seeking greater economic development, better housing grants, and speedier progress on land claims. Some progress is being made: the government recently handed over a significant chunk of Northwest Territory, and negotiations continue over the Queen Charlotte Islands.

One positive result of the Oka confrontation, according to Mohawk teacher Mary Nicholas, is "a new awareness of our language, our culture, who we are." She teaches at the Mohawk-immersion elementary school located only a few hundred yards from the spot of the 1990 barricade. The school's name, Rotiwennenkehte, reflects the new search for Mohawk identity; it translates roughly as "People have the responsibility for carrying on the language." Mary Nicholas explained proudly, "The voice of the land is in the language."

The symbols of the peace tree painted on a wall at the school reflect the Mohawk reverence for the natural world. On the lower branches of the tree are the "life-sustainers" (corn, beans, and squash); thunder is called "our grand-father"; the moon is "our grandmother"; the sun is "our elder brother"; and the very top of the tree is "the seat of the creator." These kinship names remind humans to treat all parts of nature with the same love and respect that they would treat their own relatives.

*A Navajo at work in a reservation lumber mill. Today Indians struggle to provide employment for their people without over-exploiting their natural resources.*

as $20 million a month. Indians are using this money to build better housing and to create cultural awareness programs in their schools; many tribes are investing their income as well. Such income, independent of government sources, furthers Indian self-determination. But casinos may also create some new problems for the tribes: already there are concerns as to whether gambling runs contrary to some tribal values.

The exploitation of natural resources is another major concern because Indian lands are some of the last areas with abundant forests and rich mineral resources. Native Americans are under constant pressure to develop their land to create jobs for their people. Yet they must also balance practical concerns with traditional spiritual values. As more people in today's fast-paced world search for meaning, there has been renewed respect for native culture and for the truths upon which it is based. The tribal integrity of Native Americans, as well as their belief in the sacredness of the Earth and Sky, continue to grow stronger with the passage of time.

# MODERN-DAY WOMEN WARRIORS

Contrary to their Hollywood image as meek, docile wives who are subordinate to men, Indian women have formed the core of resistance to genocide and colonization throughout history. In addition to their roles as caretakers and nurturers, they have been the backbone of their people.

JoAnn Tall, an Oglala Lakota mother of eight, has followed a long tradition in resisting the exploitation of her people. Last April the San Francisco–based Goldman Environmental Foundation awarded her $60,000 as one of 1993's seven "environmental heroes" from around the world who have, despite extreme hardships, committed themselves to grassroots activism.

Tall's activism spans more than twenty years; she was chosen for her efforts to organize against toxic waste dumps and nuclear weapons testing on Indian lands. According to Valerie Taliman of *Ms.* magazine, Tall was quick to state that "there are a lot of strong women doing this work that you never hear about...yet they continue."

When the powerful waste industry discovered that fewer regulations govern toxic waste on Indian reservations than on land under state, county, and municipal jurisdictions, they began offering deals disguised as "economic development" to poverty-stricken tribes. By targeting communities where language barriers exist, the waste merchants did not have to worry about the translators' inability to explain the magnitude of the dangers. With no word for dioxins, PCBs, or other poisons in many Native American languages, the high-tech rhetoric makes the million-dollar waste deals sound safe.

Tall cofounded the National Resource Coalition, which joined other grassroots groups in 1991 to host a national environmental conference in the sacred Black Hills. Outraged by the idea that tribal lands were being selected as dumping grounds, they set as their goal to alert tribes to environmental racism and economic blackmail directed at Native American peoples, who retain only 4 percent of United States land. Tall helped to create the Indigenous Environmental Network at this gathering. The network now includes more than fifty organizations that are helping to educate and protect Native peoples in the United States and Canada.

Tall explains that her dedication to environmental work is based on the Lakota reverence for Grandmother Earth (Unci Maka), who has sustained her children throughout time and who must be treated with the same respect and love. Guided by a spiritual commitment that came to her in dreams and in Lakota ceremonies, Tall defended her people's rights at Wounded Knee in 1973. During this armed occupation, elder Oglala women led a resistance movement against United States domination over tribal government, lands, and rights.

Many native women continue to lead their people against the destruction of native lands caused by government and industry strip-mining, coal-burning power plants, intensive logging, and more than eight hundred nuclear bombs that exploded as "tests." Valerie Taliman, a Diné (Navajo), is an environmental writer and regular correspondent for several native publications. Juaneno/Yaqui scholar M. Annette Jaines has chronicled the history of native women's resistance to foreign domination. The Dann sisters of Nevada stood firm in their fight to save Western Shoshone homelands. Still others—such as the Navajo grandmothers fighting relocation at Big Mountain, Arizona, and the Onondaga clan mothers in New York struggling against James Bay Hydro—remain unsung heroines as they persevere on the front lines.

*Shoshone elder and well-known activist Carrie Dann.*

## » RESOURCES «

The following books contain listings of tribal addresses, phone numbers, statistics, and, in some cases, powwows and events. Contact state or provincial offices of tourism for information regarding schedules of events within the state or province and on Indian reservations.

*America's Fascinating Indian Heritage.* Pleasantville, N.Y.: The Reader's Digest Association, Inc., 1984.

Eagle/Walking Turtle. *Indian America: A Traveler's Companion.* 2nd ed. Santa Fe, N.Mex.: John Muir Publications, 1991.

Frazier, Gregory W. *The American Indian Index.* Denver: Arrowstar Publishing, 1985.

Klein, Barry T. *Reference Encyclopedia of the American Indian.* 6th ed. West Nyack, N.Y.: Todd Publications, 1992.

Leitch, Barbara A. *A Concise Dictionary of Indian Tribes of North America.* Algonac, Mich.: Reference Publications, Inc., 1979.

Mather, Christine. *Native America: Arts, Traditions, and Celebrations.* New York: Clarkson Potter Publishers, 1990.

Paisano, Edna, Joan Greendeer-Lee, June Crowles, and Debbie Carroll. *American Indian and Alaska Native Areas: 1990.* Washington, D.C.: Racial Statistics Branch, Bureau of the Census, 1991.

Waldman, Carl. *Atlas of the North American Indian.* New York: Facts on File, 1985.

## » FURTHER READING «

Beck, Peggy V., and Anna L. Walters. *The Sacred: Ways of Knowledge, Sources of Life.* Tsaile, Ariz.: Navajo Commmunity Press, 1977.

*Between Sacred Mountains: Navajo Stories and Lessons from the Land.* Tucson, Ariz.: Sun Tracks/University of Arizona Press, 1982.

Brown, Joseph Epes. *The Spiritual Legacy of the American Indian.* New York: Crossroads, 1982.

Buerge, David. *Chief Seattle.* Seattle: Sasquatch Books, 1992.

Cronyn, George W. *American Indian Poetry: An Anthology of Songs and Chants.* New York: Ballantine Books, 1972.

Esbensen, Barbara Juster. *The Star Maiden: An Ojibway Tale.* Boston: Little, Brown and Co., 1988.

Gillmor, Frances. *Windsinger.* Albuquerque, N.Mex.: Zia Books, 1976.

Goble, Paul. *The Girl Who Loved Wild Horses.* New York: Aladdin Books, 1982.

*The Handbook of North American Indians.* Washington, D.C.: U.S. Government Printing Office, 1983-90.

LaFarge, Oliver. *Laughing Boy.* New York: New American Library, 1971.

McLuhan, T.C. *Touch the Earth: A Self-Portrait of Indian Existence.* New York: Outerbridge and Dienstfrey, 1971.

Monroe, Jean Guard, and Ray Williamson. *They Dance in the Sky: Native American Star Myths.* Boston: Houghton Mifflin Company, 1987.

Nerburn, Kent, and Louise Menglekoch, eds. *Native American Wisdom.* San Rafael, Calif.: New World Library, 1991.

O'Dell, Scott. *Sing Down the Moon.* New York: Dell Publishing, 1970.

Pitts, Paul. *Racing the Sun.* New York: Avon Books, 1988.

Salmon, Julian H. *The Book of Indian Crafts and Lore.* New York: Harper and Brothers, 1928.

*The World of the American Indian.* Washington, D.C.: National Geographic Society, 1974.

## » CREDITS «

# PHOTOGRAPHY AND ILLUSTRATIONS CREDITS

**INTRODUCTION and CONTENTS**
FPG: © Ferenz Fedor Studios/FPG: 2; © Jay Lurie/FPG: 15; © Jonathan A. Meyers/FPG: 16 (inset)
AP/WIDE WORLD PHOTOS: © John P. Filo/AP/Wide World: 4
AMERICAN MUSEUM OF NATURAL HISTORY: Rodman Wanamaker/AMNH, neg. #317145: 5
© Charles Mann: 6
© Stephen Trimble: 7, 8
THE FIELD MUSEUM OF NATURAL HISTORY: The Field Museum, neg. #19850, Chicago: 9 (top)
ARCHIVE PHOTOS: © Kean/Archive Photos: 9 (bottom); Archive Photos: 10, 12
ART RESOURCE: Painting by Charles Deas/Art Resource: 11
NATIONAL MUSEUM OF THE AMERICAN INDIAN/SMITHSONIAN INSTITUTION: Painting by Maxime Gachupin/NMAI: 13 (top); National Museum of the American Indian: 16
© Kirk Condyles/Impact Visuals: 13 (bottom)
© Grey Crawford: 14 (top)
© John Running: 14 (bottom)
NORTH WIND PICTURE ARCHIVE: 17

**CHAPTER 1**
AMERICAN MUSEUM OF NATURAL HISTORY: AMNH, neg. #320374: 20-21, 23 (top); R. Lenskjold/AMNH, neg. #36346: 30 (bottom); Painting by Jansson/AMNH: 33
BETTMANN NEWSPHOTOS: The Bettmann Archive: 23 (bottom)
ART RESOURCE: National Museum of American Art, Washington, D.C./Art Resource, NY: 24 (both), 26, 41
Sculpture by Cleveland Sandy, Onondaga/Iroquois Indian Museum, Howes Cave, NY: 25
NATIONAL MUSEUM OF THE AMERICAN INDIAN/SMITHSONIAN INSTITUTION: © Joseph Keppler/NMAI: 28 © Carmelo Guadagno/NMAI: 32 (top); NMAI: 32 (bottom)
NORTH WIND PICTURE ARCHIVE: 29, 30 (top), 35, 38, 39
FPG: © Paul Thompson/FPG: 31; © Leonard Lee Rue III/FPG: 36; FPG: 42
ARCHIVE PHOTOS: 40
AMERICAN MUSEUM OF NATURAL HISTORY: R.P. Sheridan/AMNH: 44
© J. Kirk Condyles: 45

**CHAPTER 2**
AMERICAN MUSEUM OF NATURAL HISTORY: AMNH, neg. #116808: 46-47, 49 (top)
EASTERN NATIONAL; © Eastern National: 49 (bottom), 50 (bottom); © Michael Bitsko/Eastern National: 50 (top)
ART RESOURCE: © Giraudon/Art Resource: 52
ARCHIVE PHOTOS: 53
NORTH WIND PICTURE ARCHIVE: 55, 60
FPG: FPG: 54, 62 (top); © Jay Lurie/FPG: 57 (bottom) © Willie Hill/FPG: 59 (left)
BETTMANN NEWSPHOTOS: The Bettmann Archive: 56; Painting by Robert Lindneux/The Bettmann Archive: 58
© John Running: 59 (right)
PUBLIC DOMAIN: 57 (top), 62 (bottom)
NATIONAL MUSEUM OF THE AMERICAN INDIAN/SMITHSONIAN INSTITUTION: © Frank G. Speck/NMAI: 63

**CHAPTER 3**
FPG: 64–65, 67 (top), 95 (bottom)
AMERICAN MUSEUM OF NATURAL HISTORY: George Catlin/AMNH: 67 (bottom); G.L. Wilson/AMNH, neg. #286503: 70; AMNH: 72 (bottom); Rodman Wanamaker/AMNH, neg. #316691; Logan/AMNH: 84; Adam Anik/AMNH: 90
© Sandra Wavrick: 71, 82
SUPERSTOCK: Painting by W.R. Leigh, Whitney Gallery of Western Art, Cody, WY/Superstock: 72 (top)
THE BETTMANN ARCHIVE: 73
ARCHIVE PHOTOS: Archive Photos/American Stock: 75; Archive Photos: 76 (bottom)
WYOMING STATE MUSEUM: 78
ART RESOURCE: National Museum of American Art, Washington, D.C./Art Resource, NY: 68; Painting by Nick Eggenhofer/Art Resource, NY: 76 (top); © Werner Forman Archive, Smithsonian Institution, Washington, D.C./Art Resource, NY: 79 (bottom); © Werner Forman Archive, Field Museum of Natural History, Chicago/Art Resource, NY: 81 (bottom); George Catlin/National Museum of American Art, Washington, D.C./Art Resource, NY: 83 (left); © Werner Forman Archive, Museum of the American Indian, Heye Foundation, NY/Art Resource: 83 (right); Painting by John Clymer, NEFSKY/Art Resource, NY: 85
NATIONAL MUSEUM OF THE AMERICAN INDIAN/SMITHSONIAN INSTITUTION: NMAI: 79 (top)
© John Running: 86
PHOTOFEST: 87
AP/WIDE WORLD PHOTOS: 88 (top)
© Richard Riddell: 88 (bottom)
© David F. Barry/Amon Carter Museum, Fort Worth, TX: 89
© Greta Pratt: 91

**CHAPTER 4**
NORTH WIND PICTURE ARCHIVE: 92–93, 95 (top)
FPG: FPG: 95 (bottom); © Thompson of Albuquerque/FPG: 102; © Henry Miller/FPG: 105, 106; © Bill Reasons/FPG: 110
AMERICAN MUSEUM OF NATURAL HISTORY: R.H. Lowie/AMNH, neg.#118646: 96; R.H. Lowie/AMNH, neg. #11683: 99; © Don Eiler/AMNH: 103 (bottom); J.K. Dixon/AMNH, neg. #317348; Rodman Wanamaker/AMNH, neg. #316892: 107; R.H. Lowie/AMNH, neg. #1188803: 108; Rodman Wanamaker/AMNH, neg. #316891: 109
© Stephen Trimble: 97
© David Stoecklein: 98
© Bob Pool/Tom Stack and Associates: 103 (top)
THE BETTMANN ARCHIVE: 112, 114
© Frank Oberle/Tony Stone Worldwide: 115

**CHAPTER 5**
AMERICAN MUSEUM OF NATURAL HISTORY: E.S. Curtis/AMNH, neg. #335538: 116–117, 119 (top); O. Bauer/P. Hollenbeak/AMNH, neg. #337569: 119 (bottom); © A. Singer/AMNH: 120 (top); AMNH, neg. #337824: 123; © AMNH: 124, 125; AMNH, neg. #330387: 126; E.W. Merrill/AMNH, neg. #328742: 127; AMNH, neg. #11214: 128; © AMNH ("Objects of Bright Pride"): 129 (top); © AMNH: 129 (bottom); AMNH, neg. #328740: 130; © Lee Boltin/AMNH: 131; AMNH, neg. #34583: 132; J.K. Dixon/AMNH, neg. #317060: 133
© John Running: 120 (bottom)
© John Isaac: 122
THE FIELD MUSEUM OF NATURAL HISTORY: neg. #A108441C, Chicago: 126 (silhouette)

**CHAPTER 6**
NATIONAL MUSEUM OF THE AMERICAN INDIAN/SMITHSONIAN INSTITUTION: NMAI: 134–135, 137 (top); © Edward Brooks/NMAI: 139; Paul Warner Collection/NMAI: 142; © Edward H. Davis/NMAI: 143; NMAI: 145
AMERICAN MUSEUM OF NATURAL HISTORY: Painting by Jansson/AMNH: 137 (bottom); J.K. Dixon/AMNH, neg. #317171: 138; R.P. Sheridan/AMNH: 141 (top); J.K. Dixon/AMNH, neg. #317044: 144
NORTH WIND PICTURE ARCHIVE: 140, 146
© Stephen Trimble: 141 (bottom)
FPG: 147

**CHAPTER 7**
FPG: FPG: 148–149, 151 (top); © Bowerman/FPG: 153 (bottom); © Jack Breed/FPG: 154; © Ferenz Fedor Studios/FPG: 161, 165 (bottom); © Herb & Dorothy McLaughlin/FPG: 166 (bottom); National Archives/FPG: 168; © Frank Meitz/FPG: 171; © Jonathan A. Meyers/FPG: 175 (bottom)
NORTH WIND PICTURE ARCHIVE: 151 (bottom)
ARCHIVE PHOTOS: Archive Photos: 152, 160, 162, 173; Archive Photos/American Stock: 156; © Esther Henderson/Archive Photos: 167
© Stephen Trimble: 153 (top), 157 (top), 158, 169 (right), 175 (top)
© John Running: 155, 165 (top), 172 (top)
© Michael Chiago/The Heard Museum, Phoenix, AZ: 157 (bottom)
AP/WIDE WORLD PHOTOS: © Sam Levitz/AP/Wide World Photos: 159; © Kenji Kawano/AP/Wide World Photos: 164
© Grey Crawford: 166 (top), 174 (left)
© Lois Ellen Frank: 169 (left)
© Robert C. Dawson/F-Stock Photos: 170
© Charles Mann: 172 (bottom), 174 (right)

**EPILOGUE:**
© Elijah Cobb: 176
FPG: © Leo D. Harris/FPG: 177; © FPG: 180; © Herb & Dorothy McLaughlin/FPG: 186
BETTMANN NEWSPHOTOS: The Bettmann Archive: 178 (top); UPI/Bettmann: 179, 182, 184 (top)
ARCHIVE PHOTOS: 178 (bottom)
IMPACT VISUALS: © J. Kirk Condyles: 181; © Ronnie Farley/Impact Visuals: 185 (bottom); © Kirk Condyles/Impact Visuals: 187
© John Isaac: 185

**All maps:** © Cameron Clement, 1994
**All drawings:** © Steve Arcella, 1994: 27, 34, 51,

# ≫ INDEX ≪